ADRIAN LANGENSCHEID

FINLAND TRUE CRIME

HARROWING SHORT STORIES ABOUT MURDER, ROBBERY, KIDNAPPING, ABUSE, AND THEFT

About this book:

Ice-cold serial killers, doomed family dramas, tragic kidnappings, vile torture, and unscrupulous abuse: fourteen shocking True Crime short stories based on true crime cases from Finland.

Captivated, stunned, amazed, and moved to tears, you will question everything you thought you knew about human nature. Life scripts horrifying stories and this book sums them up. Dive into the shocking world of true crime and real criminal cases!

About the author:

Adrian Langenscheid is the author of the successful True Crime International book series. As a passionate true crime expert, Adrian is mentioned in the same breath as German true crime greats such as Harbort, Benecke, or Tsokos. His books have achieved bestseller status beyond Germany's borders. The sixth book in the series follows on from the remarkable success of its predecessors. Together with his wife and children, Adrian lives on the edge of the Black Forest, Baden-Württemberg.

Content

ADRIAN LANGENSCHEID

HARROWING SHORT STORIES ABOUT MURDER, ROBBERY, KIDNAPPING, ABUSE, AND THEFT

Imprint

Authors: Adrian Langenscheid, Lisa Bielec, Marie van den Boom, Fabian Maysenhölder, Heike Schlosser

ISBN:
978-3-98661-084-5 Finnland True Crime Engl. Paperback

Translation: Lea Prescher

1st edition February 2023
© 2023 Stefan Waidelich, Zeisigweg 6, 72212 Altensteig, Germany.
Cover image: © Canva (canva.com)
Cover design: Pixa Heros, Stuttgart

Preface

These last two years have been full of surprises for me. Without any expectations and born out of a passionate interest in true crime, I published the books "True Crime USA", "True Crime England", "True Crime Sweden", and "True Crime France" after the successful debut of my first book, "True Crime Germany". All have become bestsellers within the True Crime genre and still months later, all are still on the bestseller's lists, thanks to the support of my numerous readers. They have been translated into English as well as Spanish and recorded as audio books.

The unexpected success and public response continue to humble me because, looking back, there are things I would have done differently with my first two books. It is my passion to write and publish books, however, I am very aware that this would not have been possible without you, my dear readers. For this, my thanks go out to each of you. Thank you for your honest reviews and feedback. I read each and every one, take them all to heart, and am thrilled to receive such positive reviews. With "Finland True Crime," you now hold the sixth book in the series in your hands. It is with gratitude that I dedicate it to you and everyone else who has contributed to the success of this book series with their purchase, feedback, and reviews.

Thank you!

All the best,

Adrian Langenscheid

Introduction

There she sat, screaming so loudly that all eyes in the room turned to us. If her wrinkled hands had not clasped mine with such an energetic grip, I would have walked away. The situation was more than unpleasant for me. Her eyes looked at me intently and in broken German she furiously stated: "You don't do things like that! You don't do things like that?!" Each time she became louder and more emphatic. Her voice reverberated in the somewhat sterile-looking group room. A tear slowly ran down Devora's cheek. Then another. It was a burst of emotions that threatened to overwhelm me. Nearly half a century had passed, but she was crying as if it were yesterday.

It was the year 2004, andI was far from home in Haifa. Together with other young adults, I had embarked on a "peace tour" that had taken us to the north of Israel, among other places, to this home for Holocaust survivors. Many people were there. The tattooed numbers on their arms half-faded but still visible, as were the memories. We were greeted extraordinarily kindly in broken German by a Holocaust survivor. You could hear the Yiddish in his voice as he greeted us with his carefully pre-written text. Our message to these people was clear: Germany is not as you remember it. We are sorry! We sang a song and distributed roses afterwards.

It was hereere that I met Devora. While she continued to hold my hand tightly, she told me her moving story… about the concentration camp…about how she lost her whole family when she was 14 years old…and about how she was all alone after the war ended. Her eyes spoke volumes of grief. Like clouds of mist, she was surrounded by the old pain and despair over the fate that had befallen her. She also told me about the commander who called them all pigs - They would all be worth nothing more than pigs. That was the moment when she screamed, "You don't do things like that, you don't do things like that?!"

It seemed to me that I was not holding the hand of this old, sad, and bitter woman, but that of the 14-year-old girl of that time - trapped in the past and still deeply connected to her long-dead tormentors. Pushed through by anger, bitterness, and contempt, cursed to revisit the humiliations of days gone by over and over again - this crime scarred them forever.

As I glanced around at the other Holocaust survivors, some of whom were cordial and joking with my friends, a crystal-clear thought came to me full of pity: "If only you had managed to forgive, you could have had a happy life." I did not utter the thought because I was ashamed of it.

Who am I to allow myself to make such a judgment in the face of such suffering? What if such a cruel lot were assigned to me? Would I ever find hope and peace again after such a terrible blow of fate? Could I forgive and get back on my feet or would some fledgling sit in front of me after many agonizing years and pass judgment?

As my gaze wandered among the survivors in that home - they seemed happy. I began to feel that we could recover even from humanity's most horrific crimes, but then I looked into the dark teary eyes of Devora and knew - not everyone.

The glimpse beyond the ideal world that I caught in 2004 moves me to this day and, along with several other experiences, is why I invest a lot of time in researching crimes. I can only shake my head in disbelief at the depth of human abysses that are often hidden behind bourgeois facades.

Life sometimes writes stories that leave protagonists and viewers stunned and shocked. The descriptions in this book do not come from the imagination of a writer. It is the cruel reality that confronts you in the next fourteen chapters. It is a reality more harrowing than any fiction, with people - like Devora - left stunned and broken, depicting victims who are forced to either face the suffering they have endured or perish.

This book will introduce you to more criminal cases, this time from Finland. These are tales in short story form, authentic and close to reality, about crimes that actually happened - and not so long ago. One could write a whole book about each case with deep psychological analysis, but that is not my intention. Short stories are like an unexpected storm - before you know it, it's over. What remains is the question that victims inevitably face, often for the rest of their lives: Why?

These are crimes in short form that make you empathize and think. Let yourself be pulled into the depths of the human abyss by a variety of murder cases, abuse, desecration of corpses, cannibalism, kidnapping, blackmail, lies, intrigue, and manipulation. You will be shocked, as I was.

Devora is no longer alive, but I sometimes still see her, tearyeyed, standing before me.

CHAPTER 1

Good night, my darling

"Good night, my darling." Helvi affectionately kisses her grandson on the forehead. An audio cassette is playing in the background, but the story won't slowly and quietly lull the child to sleep. Helvi turns up the volume. For her, the cassette is the only way to drown out the screams, crying, and wailing that blast from the living room. She doesn't live far from her daughter and helps out almost daily when her son-in-law wants to sort out his relationship problems in his own unique way. She fervently hopes that the adventurous stories about Pipi Longstocking and Michel from Lönneberga will captivate her grandson so he can fall asleep distracted. But little Oskar is a clever child who had to grow up far too early. He already knows, at the age of six, that it is his mommy who is crying in pain and despair. He also knows the reason for her suffering: his father. He is the one who hits her, kicks her, and yells at her. Oskar doesn't understand why and in the end, doesn't care because he knows one thing for sure: "Good night, Grandma. One day, I'm going to kill Daddy."

Esko is three years old when a friendly, smiling woman comes to their home and takes him with her. She wants to take his little brother, Matthi, and him to a new home. Esko doesn't ask any questions. He thinks it has something to do with Mummy. Frequently, men he doesn't know come by and do strange things to her. They yell at her, hit her, and lay on top of her. After a few minutes, the men make funny noises and get up. They give mom money or little plastic bags of white powder that look like sherbet. Esko would have liked to try some of it, but Mummy always says it's not good for him. They now sit in the woman's car and Esko wonders what the powder would have tasted like. Their little suitcases are safely tucked away in the trunk. She had to make him a solemn promise to take good care of the luggage after all, he was only allowed to take his favorite things with him - he wouldn't want to lose them under any circumstances.

The home to which the woman from Youth Welfare takes Esko and Matthi is really nothing more than a roof over their heads. Throughout their young lives, the woman continually comes by, taking them to new homes, to new people. In their teens, the two boys finally return to their mother. The men who come in and out are still there and the little bags of white powder are still lying around everywhere in the apartment but by now, Esko knows it is not sherbet. He understands that his mother is a prostitute and a drug addict. Money is always tight, and the refrigerator always empty. Esko can't stand the look on his brother Matthi's face, who is two years younger. "I'm hungry," he says quietly, even in the morning after getting up, if once again there was no meal on the table the night before. Esko knows every supermarket in town inside and out, so he knows that the old owner of the small grocery store around the corner won't notice if he steals a few apples. She doesn't, however, have any hot, pre-cooked meals so he needs to get those from the big supermarket chain. Here, he has to be very careful because the company can afford security personnel. Already caught more than once, he explains that the food is for his brother who is hungry, but no one is interested in the truth. The guards report him to the police, who sentence him to community service or juvenile detention.

At school, there is no one Esko can call a friend. His classmates throw paper balls at him and make fun of his worn-out clothes and unkempt hair. In these situations, Esko lashes out. His teachers see him as the mastermind and aggressor. They are only interested in his poor grade point average, not the reasons for it, but Esko's interest in school is limited anyway. He tells himself that as soon as his compulsory basic training is behind him, he will leave this miserable town and everyone and everything behind, taking only Matthi and Ulla with him. Ulla is 15 years old, two years younger than Esko. He first notices her in the schoolyard when some classmates push her and laugh at her. Esko intervenes, and since then the two are more than just young in love - they are a team. Ulla and Esko, Esko and Ulla against the rest of the world. The two can only see each other on the weekends, as Esko took a job as a parking attendant after graduating from school. When he is with his girlfriend, he becomes a completely different person and listens to her attentively. Everything Ulla says intrigues him tremendously. When she is 16 years old, the two move into a small, rented apartment in a village two hours away from their home. They were only able to sign the lease with the help of Helvi, Ulla's mother, because Ulla is still a minor. A year later, she becomes pregnant with Esko's child. Little Oskar is her sunshine. The young mother loves her son more than anything and has since she was allowed to hold him in her arms for the first time after his birth. She is concerned about the developments in their relationship.

Esko does not seem interested in his son. He drinks - at first only in the evening with his friends, then increasingly during the day as well. The men he calls his buddies are shady guys without jobs, addicted to drugs and alcohol. Esko, too, loses every job he starts within a few weeks. This leaves Ulla to look for a job to provide for Oskar. Helvi also helps the young family. She touchingly takes care of her grandson when Ulla is at work in a factory and Esko is lying on the sofa, drunk. Under the influence of heavy drinking, Esko's mood changes in a matter of seconds. He yells at Ulla if she serves him the wrong food or wears clothes he feels are inappropriate. He sometimes pushes her or firmly grabs her by the arm. Afterwards, he apologizes in tears and promises to do better.

When Oskar is four months old, Esko chokes Ulla. She awaits the evening until he has gone out with his drinking buddies, then quickly packs up Oskar's and her most important clothes and flees to her mother's house. Helvi is shocked. She knew that Esko had a drinking problem and violent mood swings, but the choking is a definite step too far. She is relieved that her daughter drew a line to keep her grandson and herself safe, but Esko does not accept the separation.

During the day when Helvi goes to work, he sneaks around outside her house. He shouts loudly for Ulla to open the door, saying she cannot forbid him to see his son, but Ulla remains strong. Esko alternates between romantic professions of love, remorseful apologies, lofty promises to make everything better, threats, and insults. After a few days, he relies only on apologies and promises, and Ulla grows weak. She opens the door to Esko, but Helvi refuses to be fooled. That same evening when she comes home, she firmly asks her son-in-law to leave or she would inform the police. Helvi has kept a pistol in a drawer in the living room closet for years – because you just never know. What she didn't know until now, however, is that Esko knows where it is hidden. After Helvi threatens him with the police, he unerringly reaches into the drawer, pulls out the pistol, and shoots indiscriminately. Helvi has the presence of mind to duck and shouts to Ulla to get Oskar and herself to safety. Her grandson cries bitterly, as his fear is abundantly clear. Over the last few days, he had been such a calm and even-tempered child. He slept through the nights, ate his porridge decently, and often laughed with her. The thought that with Esko, trouble, sadness, and violence are now complicating his young life again, causes Helvi to burst into tears. Esko laughs, drops the gun, and leaves the living room.

A few days later, Ulla and Esko rent an apartment a few streets away, next to the house of her sister, Karin. Helvi begs her daughter to get help, but Ulla loves Esko, claiming "He will get better, mom. He promised us, Oskar and me." But Esko does not change.

Years pass and Ulla is caught in a spiral of physical violence and psychological terror. Esko steals Ulla's money, and when she has none left, he becomes aggressive. One evening, in the apartment next to Karin, he punches Ulla in the face so hard that she loses an incisor and her eardrum bursts. After this incident, Ulla desperately turns to her sister and her sister's husband. They try to find Esko, but he is a master at disappearing and hiding undetectably. No one knows where he stays after escapades like these. A pattern develops of violent separations, subsequent moves to new apartments, and returns to Esko. The latter serves more and more time in prison for violent crimes and drug offenses. During these times, Ulla moves in with Helvi or into a new apartment - desperate attempts to get away from Esko, but he writes her letters from prison with apologies and professions of love so Ulla keeps telling him her new address. Helvi is also unable to stand up to her daughter's partner. Several times he smashes her windows with large stones and climbs up the water pipe to force his way into her house. The police, too, can rarely do anything about Esko unless charges are filed against him.

Ulla desperately clings to the good moments. When Esko is not drunk, he takes care of Oskar and is a loving partner. While in custody he gets a capsule inserted into his arm that makes him extra sensitive to alcohol so he can no longer drink. For a few days, the three of them lead an almost normal life. They go on a camping trip and Esko finds a new job in a timber factory. But after a few days, Esko argues with his supervisor and staples him to the worktable with a nail gun. That same evening, Ulla notices a wound on Esko's arm and that he is reaching for the bottle again.

In November 1993, Ulla and Esko get married. He assured her that he would get better if only they were finally married. He promises to get sober, stop hitting her, get a job, and spend time with his son. The two move into Esko's apartment after the wedding, and shortly thereafter into a new, slightly larger apartment on the third floor of another apartment building. After a few weeks, however, Ulla realizes that once again it was just empty promises. She informs Oskar that they will be moving out and Oskar remains silent. He is about the same age now as Ulla was when she met Esko. Early on, the boy understood that his father was an alcoholic tyrant. More and more often, he forces his son to ride along on his tours and collect money for him. Last week, Oskar had to beat and kick a man so bad he needed a hospital. He didn't want to, but his father threatened to kill Ulla and him if he refused. Oskar loves his mother, but he can' t count the moves anymore. He can' t stand the back and forth but he says nothing. Instead, he packs his suitcases. Ulla also hastily stuffs some clothes into her travel bag, but Esko returns home earlier that evening than she had hoped. The two argue and when Ulla yells, "I'm going to divorce you!", Esko grabs a knife. He uses it to block her from the front door. While Oskar sits in his room waiting for the two of them to make up, as they often do, his mother runs away from the front door, towards the balcony. She climbs over the railing and is now stuck on the third floor, several meters above the ground. Esko says nothing, standing petrified behind the balcony door, the knife clutched tightly in his hand. "Mommy!" shouts Oskar. "Run to grandma, sweetie, I'll catch up," his mother gasps. She tries to shimmy her way to the neighbor's balcony, but it is freezing cold as the Finnish winter has already set in. Ulla is wearing neither a jacket nor gloves. The railing of the balcony is iced over, and darkness falls on the night. Outside, you can hardly see anything. Oskar finally understands what is happening a few seconds later but can do nothing to stop this cruel moment. His mother slips and falls - from the third floor into the snow. Crying, Oskar bends down and calls to her. He sees her move and stunned, yells for help, running all over and ringing every doorbell as Esko disappears into the night.

At the hospital, the doctor is amazed to see Ulla standing upright. She has not suffered any serious injuries, not even a broken bone. After the incident, Helvi gives her the keys to a remote cabin in the forest. Owned by the family for centuries, it has no electricity, no running water, no grid - and no Esko. The tyrant knows nothing about this hut. It is not a long-term solution, that much is clear to everyone. Ulla can't call in sick to work forever, and Oskar has to go to school. The two stay in the forest for a week - seven restful, quiet days. When they return, luck is on their side as Esko is not there. They learn from Helvi that he is once again in custody. The two use the time to move - for the last time. Ulla files for divorce after six months of marriage.

A few weeks later, during recess at school, Oskar notices that he is laughing. He can't remember the last time he had that feeling in his stomach. This is what fun feels like. He is chatting with his best friend and his thoughts no longer revolve around his mother's black eye, or his father's alcoholic fumes or loud buddies keeping him up at night. Oskar's friend also notices the change and is pleased because he doesn't quickly break off the conversation again, as usual, but tells Oskar at length about his new computer game. But suddenly he stops in the middle of his sentence and looks past Oskar with a frightened expression. The latter now feels a hand on his shoulder and smells alcohol-soaked breath. "Where's your mom?"

Oskar had to tell him. What else could he do? Let the situation escalate? His father was completely drunk, and his strong hands were holding him so tightly that he knew exactly what he was in for if he didn't cooperate. Besides his best friend, he had few other classmates he got along with. He didn't want to lose that one good relationship by having his friend see what kind of person his father was. And so, that same evening, all of his mother's facial features derail when she sees her ex-husband sitting on the couch. He is back and he has come to stay.

Ulla doesn't blame her son for giving Esko her new address. She knows how scary he can be. Their happiness only lasted a few months, but it was a good time and she is grateful for the little peace and quiet they got. But Ulla now gives up, as she no longer has the strength to fight her ex-husband.

He asks for money more and more often - money that Ulla does not have. When she returns home from the supermarket on September 14, 1995, carrying two heavy shopping bags, Esko and his gang are already gathered in the living room. The air is stuffy, smelling of cigarettes and beer. Loud music makes the walls shake. "We're hungry," slurs one of the unkempt, burly men, approaching them. Instinctively, Ulla takes a step back, but he's not after her, he's after the groceries. Within a few minutes, the group has looted most of their freshly bought food. While 20 Finnish marks remain in Ulla's wallet, she soon loses them after less than an hour in her own home. Esko wants to go out to a bar with his friends, and they need the money for that. Ulla feels nothing at all since his return. Her face is white, her eyes empty. It is as if all of her life's energy has been drained from her. Without saying a word, she hands him the 20-mark bill but Esko just laughs and throws the bill at her feet. "What am I supposed to do with 20 marks?" Again, Ulla responds without objecting. She picks up the phone and dials her parents' number. Her father picks up and she asks him for money. "Is it that Esko again who is bothering you and pushing you to do this?" he asks angrily. Mechanically, in a low voice, Ulla denies it. She informs her ex-husband that she will get the money from her father and bring it to the bar.

Together with Oskar, Ulla sets off for her parents' house. Her father left after her call. Her situation was causing him a lot of trouble, Helvi explains to her daughter as she gives her a bundle of bills. Ulla leaves the house and drives off with Oskar. She stops at an ATM and withdraws her entire bank balance. Arriving in front of her apartment, she hugs her son tightly. "I love you," she affirms urgently, handing him her wallet. "Give Grandpa his money back and then pay all the bills. I have something to do." Oskar is left confused as his mother sets off once again on her bicycle to visit Grandma. Helvi didn't expect to see her daughter again that day. As Ulla stands before her, the loving mother's stomach tightens and she loses her footing after the following words from her daughter, "I love you, Mom. I'm going to kill myself now."

After Oskar enters the empty apartment, he suddenly understands. His mother has said goodbye to him - forever. He tries frantically to call his grandmother, but she does not answer. At the same time, Helvi is wandering through the city in a state of total disarray, crying for her daughter. She desperately tried to stop Ulla, but she sped away on her bicycle immediately after her announcement. Helvi also informed Ulla's sister, Karin. By phone, Karin asks Oskar to stay in the apartment in case Ulla returns.

Karin is also terribly worried about her sister, but she realizes that she must now remain calm. She returns to her parents' house with her crying mother. At every port of call, someone is waiting for Ulla in case she should return. Karin places her mother at the kitchen table and sets a glass of water out for her. "I'll be right back. I'm just going to the bathroom for a minute," she says. A few cold splashes of water would certainly help her keep a clear head, but when she opens the bathroom door, all those good intentions are lost in one fell swoop, and a sharp cry escapes her.

Her sister is lying motionless on the bathroom floor. The place is in chaos. Empty jars, packages and blister packs lay everywhere. Ulla must have cycled away just for show when in reality, she returned to her parents' house and took all the tablets from the medicine cabinet at once. Karin sees that her sister is still alive, breathing heavily and slurring her words, but she is pale and seems out of it, unresponsive. Karin immediately runs back to the kitchen and calls the ambulance. She then informs Oskar, who immediately sets off. The phone is not wireless, which is why she can't stop Helvi from heading straight for the bathroom.

Karin finds her mother frozen in the doorway, shaking all over. Karin hugs Helvi and assures her that Ulla is still alive and that the emergency doctor would arrive in a few moments. Oskar, who arrived soon after, is crying, but it is not only grief that pours out of him, but also anger, and determination. "I'm going to kill him," he keeps repeating. When the ambulance arrives to take Ulla away, Helvi begs Karin and Oskar not to leave Ulla's side. She promises to follow. Karin is surprised when she sees her mother put a knife in her blue handbag and leave the house.

At just before 8 p.m., Helvi arrives at Esko's favorite bar. She sees him playing billiards with the criminal losers he calls his friends. How he laughs drunkenly and bawls as if all is right with the world. He is happy. How can he be happy when he is causing his family so much pain? She thinks about how she almost lost her daughter and Oskar almost lost his mother forever today, then she takes a deep breath and exhales calmly. Waiting for Esko to come to the bar, it doesn't take long before he orders new drinks. The gang has probably managed to find money elsewhere. "Ulla is dead," she says. Esko turns to her and replies, "Where is she?" "She's dead!" replies Helvi, louder now. The two get into an argument. As Esko turns and says, "I'm going to find Ulla," Helvi pulls the knife from her pocket and stabs him in the chest. She withstands her son-in-law's surprised look and watches him sink to the floor.

Guests scream out in shock all around. The waiters at the bar are horrified and afraid of what is about to happen. Helvi puts down the knife and at 20:16 a bartender calls the police and the emergency doctor. Helvi, meanwhile, tries to calm the witnesses. "Don't worry. He deserved to die." Slowly, she walks into the kitchen where she stays until the police arrive half an hour later. Along with them come Karin and Oskar, who were informed by the officers earlier. Her grandson looks Helvi in the eye and instinctively knows what has happened. "You can't take my grandma!" he pleads with the police. "She was just trying to protect me. I would have done it myself!" Helvi takes Oskar in her arms and smiles at him. "You don't have to worry anymore."

In custody, Helvi proves cooperative. That same evening she agrees to be questioned, but first demands to know if Esko is dead. When the investigators answer in the affirmative, Helvi internally thanks God. She describes the whole story, starting with the meeting between Esko and her then 15-year-old daughter. She recounts the violent outbursts against Ulla and their shared son, the alcohol and drug problems, the stalking, the shooting in their home and her daughter's suicide attempt. "Esko brought nothing but pain and suffering to my daughter," she says. That night, when she realized she could have lost her daughter, she had to act. She knows it is wrong to kill another human being but for her daughter and grandson, there was no way around it.

Ulla quickly recovers from her overdose. After her ex-husband's funeral, she visits his grave regularly and brings him fresh flowers every week.

The trial against Helvi begins in October 1995. First, a psychiatric report must be drawn up, which takes around six months. During this time, Helvi settles in and makes friends among the prison guards. One of the guards is Markus, with whom she gets along particularly well because of his fun-loving nature and sense of humor. The other inmates also love her. She always has an open ear, especially for the younger offenders, and soon becomes a mother figure to them. Ulla, Karin, and Oskar visit Helvi as often as prison regulations allow.

In March 1996, the result of the expert opinion is published - Helvi was not completely responsible for her actions at the time of the crime, as she had been traumatized by the near death of her daughter. This shock continued even after the certainty that Ulla was alive. Nevertheless, Helvi is aware of the gravity of her actions and wants to face the consequences. In the end, she is sentenced to three years and three months in prison for manslaughter under medically limiting circumstances. The minimum sentence for this crime is actually four years in prison.

After Helvi's imprisonment, Karin starts a petition for her. Within a week, almost the entire village signs it, including police officers and Matthi, Esko's brother. Karin sends the petition to the president, asking for mercy for her mother.

Helvi peels potatoes for dinner. She contributes to the prison and even enjoys the kitchen work. Today there are potatoes, vegetables, and fish - a meal that Ulla also loved as a child. Back then her daughter was happy in such a simple way. Helvi smiles at the thought and hopes that Ulla will finally regain her zest for life. The opening of the kitchen door brings her back to the present. "Good evening, Helvi," Markus greets her, "How about packing your bags and heading home?" Helvi drops the potato peeler. Markus is humorous, but he wouldn't joke at the expense of her history and imprisonment. Dumbfounded, she looks at him. "It's true. The president has pardoned you."

In fact, Finnish President Martti Ahtisaari approved the petition, though not publicly. Therefore, when Helvi arrives at the door that evening, Ulla bursts into tears without restraint. Her mother holds her in her arms, wanting to calm her down, but Ulla reassures her: "It's all right, Mom. This time they are tears of joy."

CHAPTER 2

The cattle breeder

The short, dry news hit like a bomb - a forced sale had been scheduled in North Karelia. It was a small, run-down summer house in the typical wooden construction, not far from an idyllic lake. Apparently, the owner had used it as a farm and kept cattle, because a milking machine of a renowned brand was explicitly mentioned in the inventory. The new owner would also acquire this machine.

The forced sale occurred due to several debts of the previous owner. Thus, there would be, for example, 28 euro debts with the electricity companies, which, among other things, were to be paid off from the auction sum. In addition, damage claims to the owner were still pending. This, however, came without further explanations.

At first sight, this appeared to be a simple forced sale. It made a big splash, however. It was not the auction content or amount owed that made it so, but rather the naming of the cattle farmer as the owner. He had become a celebrity in Finland - a celebrity of the very worst kind. Even today, this case poses a mystery. It is a mystery how such a thing could happen under the eyes of the public.

The very first bid placed in the online auction was symbolic, but it shows what people think about this perpetrator. The submitted sum amounted to 666 euros - the number of the devil.

Pekka Tapani Seppänen was born in 1965 in North Karelia, Kontiolahti. It was a year marked by upheavals. The famous British politician Winston Churchill died, in New York the black American civil rights activist Malcolm X was assassinated, and later in the year the first major battle of the Vietnam War took place. But in the far, remote north of Finland, not much of this can be felt. Pekka's father is a farmer and proves to be strict in matters of education. In case of doubt, he acts harshly, but otherwise, everything seems to be going according to plan.

As a young boy, Pekka quickly develops a special fondness and fascination for cattle. Cows have a calmness and equanimity, with their soulful, gentle eyes. At the age of eight, the boy sought opportunities to watch them, even traveling to farms in the area to be close to the animals. Nearly every day, he studies his pets and spends time with them.

The child, on the other hand, is much less enthusiastic about school - and will remain so throughout Finnish elementary school (grades 1-9). Pekka leaves school at the age of 15, immediately after finishing 9th grade. He does not attend secondary school because his career aspiration is clear: he wants to become a farmer and have a farm with dairy cattle.

Pekka pursues this goal passionately, and has a knack for cattle breeding. After some time, the 6' 1" man with the robust build and blond curls becomes a minor celebrity on the scene, winning numerous awards and prizes at shows for his cows. He collects the trophies he wins with great pride and displays them at his farm.

At some point, however, Pekka's enthusiasm for his cows seems to wane and his life turns in a different direction.

Besides cows, Pekka has another preference: he loves to swim, and he's quite good at it. So effortlessly does he trudge through the cool water, that other swimmers at the local bathing establishment point out that it's as if water is his element. Even as Pekka gets heavier and stockier over the years, he remains an excellent swimmer.

It's unclear exactly when Pekka's drinking started. He actually could have led a successfully carefree life with the numerous subsidies and farming support from Finnish funds and EU pots. In addition to his main residence, the farm in Kontiolahti, Seppänen owns another farm and has use of a summer house on a nearby lake, which belongs to his mother, though he can use it as he sees fit.

The farmer, who likes to walk around with his shirt wide open and a thick gold chain around his neck, is not popular among his neighbors or fellow citizens. Many are afraid of Pekka and try their best to avoid and not mess with him. He is also no stranger to the local police.

Over time, Seppänen develops into a person who increasingly comes into conflict with the law. These conflicts often involve traffic offenses, but later include problems with his animal husbandry. When Pekka begins to neglect his cattle, the veterinary office can no longer look the other way. Although the farmer is warned and ordered to change his husbandry conditions, he simply ignores them. Cows used to mean everything to him but now, his interest in the animals wanes more and more each year.

Instead, Seppänen increasingly turns to another source of income: alcohol, strong liquor to be more precise.

Until 2019, the handling of alcohol in Finland was very restrictive. Spirits could only be sold through a state-owned monopoly store, and prices were extremely high. Even people over the age of 22 could only purchase drinks with a maximum of 22% by volume. A desperate attempt by the government to protect the Finns from themselves - with very little success. One in 16 male Finns is an alcoholic. More than 1,000 people die of alcoholism every year, simply because they drink themselves to death.

Those who live near the border make shopping trips to neighboring countries with less stringent regulations to empty their alcohol shelves. At least, that's what Seppänen does. He regularly drives from Kontiolahti across the nearby border and buys cartons of high-proof alcohol at cheap prices, preferably vodka. Sometimes he drives up to five times a day. Seppänen drinks very little of it himself, although he does like to indulge from time to time and can take quite a lot. He thinks mainly in business terms because these purchases in Estonia or Russia, worth a total of 13,000 USD, are for his "friends."

Seppänen increasingly surrounds himself with people suffering from addictions. A large part of his entourage has alcohol problems which he exploits unscrupulously. He usually proceeds in a similar way: First, he invites the people to his home in Tohmajärvi, where they can have a drink together. In the morning, after a night of drinking, he surprisingly presents the person with a bill for the liquor he drank and he is quite insistent about payment.

Pekka simply "confiscates" the bank card of some of them and uses it to withdraw money at will. In total, it's about 9,500 USD. From one woman who can't pay, Seppänen demands that she prostitute herself. He places ads for her in the regional press, and the meetings take place in Tohmajärvi. There, the farmer owns a small front house from the 1950s, about five kilometers from the town center. He immediately takes the money from the clients - and supposedly offsets it against her debts. However, since she is heavily addicted to alcohol, she constantly needs more alcohol from Pekka Seppänen. It's a vicious circle; nevertheless, the woman is unable to bring the man to justice. From a legal standpoint this would be easy because while prostitution itself is not an offense in Finland, procuring it is severely punished and Seppänen does nothing else with her. He forces her to prostitute herself for him.

Out of fear, no one dares to rebel against Seppänen because he is absolutely ruthless in asserting his personal interests. He proves to be ice-cold, brutal, and extremely vengeful. Whoever does not submit to his will must suffer - no ifs, ands, or buts. Even torture, it is said, is one of his means of choice. Such acts are said to have occurred several times in his summer home in Viinijärvi.

In short, all of Seppänen's "friends" are dependent upon him because of their addiction problems - after all, he regularly supplies them with alcohol. They also know, from painful experience, that it is not good to resist him. That's why, in 2007, his guests at the time in the summer house in Liperi also follow him without contradiction or questions when Pekka decides to take a trip to Lake Myhkyränselä and go by rowboat to the island of Suuri-Myhkyrä. He makes demands and the visitors dutifully do what the cattleman wants. Pekka's guests, two men and two women, one of whom is his partner at the time, are drunk and poor swimmers, which he is well aware of. His partner has a cast on her leg, but she too dares not resist. Her daughter will later testify that there was a dependent relationship between Pekka and her mother, and that the farmer is to blame for the leg fracture suffered by the much younger woman.

Together, the five people walk between the closely packed trees to the jetty where the rowboat is moored. The lake lies perfectly still as all five climb into the boat, which is swaying under their weight, and carefully sit down before they cast off. With powerful strokes of the oars, the cattleman steers the rowboat out onto the lake toward the small island. With every meter the excursionists get a better view of the beautiful panoramic view. The lake is completely surrounded by tall, lush green trees. The water is smooth and silvery like a mirror, with no movement or swell to be seen. Only the small bow wave at the front of the boat churns the lake slightly. The weather is ideal for such a boat trip, and the mood of the passengers becomes increasingly exuberant and relaxed - until the unexpected happens. Suddenly and completely out of the blue, the tall, powerfully built Pekka Seppänen starts rocking the boat. He uses his entire body weight to do so, throwing himself from right to left and back again.

At first, his guests think it's a crude joke and, due to their inebriated state, don't really understand what's happening. When they do realize, they desperately, and without success, beg the cattleman to please stop! Seppänen makes the nutshell of a boat sway more and more until it gets completely out of balance and finally capsizes! Terrified and completely paralyzed by fear, the four companions plunge into the water which crashes over their heads with a loud roar.

Desperately struggling for breath, they resurface on top of the water a few moments later. All four are not good swimmers, and Seppänen's partner is also severely handicapped by her plaster leg. Panic-stricken, they try to stay afloat in a fight for survival. Anyone else would have immediately given everything to save his friends and bring them to safety, but Seppänen's reaction is ice-cold. Completely indifferent to his friends and guests, he swims single-mindedly towards the beach. Only when he notices that passers-by help his guests in their distress does he turn around and go back, but this last-minute rescue is far from the end of the matter.

When the police arrive, they are more than surprised because Seppänen is in the best of moods and even jokes around. While the four guests of the cattle farmer report excitedly and almost hysterically about the incident during questioning, Seppänen is completely relaxed and makes amusing remarks. His explanations seem quite reasonable. He confirms that it was all an accident, claiming he very rarely rides the rowboat and was therefore unable to properly operate it. This is why the boat started to sway, it eventually capsized.

Since Seppänen, with an alcohol test of 0.01 promille, is the only halfway sober individual, the policemen believe his version of the events. Despite the fact that the narrations of the scarcely rescued ones, all with a blood value between 3-4 per mille, turn out completely differently, no charges are filed and no further investigation is conducted.

A mistake? Neighbors from Tohmajärvi emphasize seeing Seppänen repeatedly on the lake in boats, so this part of his statement could easily have been checked, though no effort is made by the police officers to do so.

In 2010, just three years later, Jussi H. enters Pekka Seppänen's life and reveals another side of the farmer.

Jussi was a tall, handsome young man who happily lived with his small family. He loved his young son so much that he even had his son's name tattooed on his arm - as an eternal reminder and token of his love. Everything seemed perfect until Jussi's life suddenly came apart at the seams. One stroke of fate followed the next. First, his father died and shortly afterwards, his beloved son. For Jussi, it must have felt as if someone had pulled the rug right out from under his feet and dropped him into an endless abyss. He began drowning his grief and despair in alcohol. In the late 90s, Jussi went off the rails and committed a number of minor crimes. Finally, the formerly happy family man is convicted of burglary, payment fraud, theft, and assault. He gradually regains his composure and is waiting in a hostel for a new place of his own and the chance of a new, middle-class life when the 32-year-old meets Seppänen, who is 45 at the time.

Seppänen seems directly taken with Jussi - and, as usual, ruthlessly defies all boundaries. When the cattle farmer invites the younger man to his place to celebrate, he doesn't know what hit him. Jussi blacks out after just a few drinks and only regains consciousness after feeling a sharp pain in his body.

Seppänen had overpowered the incapacitated man and started to sexually abuse him. At Jussi's request to stop, Pekka just laughs.

From that moment on, Pekka seems to consider Jussi his property. To the outside world, everything seems as if the men have a relationship, because Jussi lives with Pekka on the farm. However, Jussi reveals to his sister that Pekka is holding him captive there. The farmer threatens him, pressures him repeatedly and even uses drugs to make the man compliant. He is raped at least one more time. Fearing Seppänen, who first checks Jussi's cell phone and later even confiscates it, he agrees on a secret code with his sister so that he can send her an encrypted call for help if necessary. But when he finally makes use of this option in his distress, it ends in a real fiasco. In May 2010, Jussi initially reports his tormentor for rape - but he withdraws the complaint a short time later. Is Seppänen putting pressure on him again? The facts recorded by the officers remain, but the incident is quickly filed away - despite the fact that the young man's relatives come to the police station in Kontiolahti at least a dozen times asking for help.

Is it possible that some of the police officers are already afraid of Pekka Seppänen at this point? One of them will admit this later. In any case, the local postal workers have been feeling the same way for a long time. Female letter carriers no longer have to go to his farm. If a package arrives for the farmer, he is called to pick it up at the post office.

Several times Jussi tries to escape, even hiding under the bed of complete strangers. But Seppänen searches entire streets for him and retrieves him. Jussi secretly tells his sister that he will then be severely "punished" for his offense.

On one occasion Jussi, who is found seriously injured, even has to go to the local hospital in Joensuu - obviously without the farmer's permission. For he shows up there with a helper. They pull the sick man out of bed and simply take him with them. A nurse calls 911 in horror, but the hospital sees no reason to act.

In return, Seppänen presents a handwritten contract between Jussi and himself, signed by Jussi himself. It states that Pekka may penetrate him "with his big cock" and "squirt his seed into my body." Although this arrangement is more than strange, the policemen do not take action even now.

A little later Jussi escapes to the local health center, from where Pekka in turn picks him up. Really voluntarily? Seppänen can later produce a text message from Jussi in which he asks him to visit him for a beer ... But what the officers do not suspect: Jussi is not in possession of this phone and Pekka has sent this message to himself. Perhaps the farmer has already decided that if he can't have Jussi, then no one else can either?

The following day, eyewitnesses see Pekka and Jussi going far out on the lake together by boat. Jussi is heavily intoxicated. Suddenly the boat begins to rock and tips over.

But apparently it can be turned around again, and the two men continue their journey for the time being. At least until the observers on the shore see that the rowboat starts rocking again and capsizes. This time, however, it continues to drift keel up.

Pekka Seppänen immediately swims towards the shore. The almost helpless Jussi is rescued by eyewitnesses. But this is of no use to him, it only postpones the already decided fate a little.

The morning after, Pekka's neighbors are abruptly roused from their sleep at around four o'clock. There is a loud argument outside by the lake! This is followed by a bloodcurdling scream, which is ended by the sound of splashing water.

Around 5:25 a.m., Pekka dials 911 and declares that Jussi is dead. He is found drowned. But the scene is more than strange, because he is lying with his head in the shallow water, while his legs are on the beach ...

This time, too, there is no further investigation. Instead, the officers advise Jussi's relatives to keep the funeral a secret so that Seppänen doesn't find out about it.

In fact, the latter makes numerous efforts to find the grave of his "partner". When he succeeds, he tears down all the floral decorations and plantings and replaces them with his own flowers. Even in death, Jussi is apparently supposed to belong to him. To him alone. Completely and totally.

In return, his fellow citizens do everything in their power to avoid the farmer and his addicts. The man spins a fatal web of economic exploitation of addicts and does not shy away from sexual violence or intimidation. He ruthlessly retaliates when someone opposes him - in whatever form. Escaping or leaving him is apparently unacceptable to Pekka, who rules over his entourage at whim like a tyrant, even forcing people into prostitution to "work off" their debts to him.

Observers of the scenes wonder why Pekka is not held accountable for years. Is it because his victims are mainly people living on the fringes of society? It is mainly alcoholics, addicts and also mentally impaired people that he has under his spell. Is it the stigma that surrounds them that prevents them from being helped? Do those involved see Seppänen's victims as second-class people, without the right to be protected by society? Or do they deliberately turn a blind eye to the suffering of the weakest in order to protect themselves? The fact is that well-off citizens, postal workers and apparently even some police officers live in fear of the farmer.

This is the only way to explain the fact that another "adventure trip" by boat in 2011 goes unpunished. This time, too, Seppänen goes out on the lake in a rowboat with two men he is friends with, accompanied by a woman. His current friend, a mentally impaired young man, is along for the ride. All appear to be heavily intoxicated. As in the first incident, Seppänen rows about a hundred meters out onto the water, then, without any notice, rocks the boat. Eventually it capsizes and his entourage falls into the water.

He himself is able to swim to the saving shore without any problems, without even glancing back at his friends who are desperately begging for help. One of them, his current partner, cannot swim. Two people can be rescued at the last minute. Some visitors boating nearby hear the panicked cries and frantic splashing of arms. They approach as quickly as they can and manage to save those fighting for survival, but Seppänen's partner drowns.

Something similar happens in July 2014, when the farmer again takes four people on a boat trip in Polijärvi. About a hundred meters from shore, he causes the boat to capsize. Three of his companions are able to save themselves ashore, like Seppänen, but the fourth drowns. In shallow water barely knee-deep.

Now, when the third person drowns in the farmer's immediate vicinity, the police begin a preliminary investigation into the numerous drowning deaths following boating accidents.

More than a year later, in 2015, Seppänen is on trial for two burglaries as well as minor alcohol offenses. Furthermore, he is fined for an animal welfare offense by the North Karelia District Court in November. He is also banned from keeping animals for two years. Recently, he had hardly taken care of his once beloved cattle. They had to vegetate in far too small, filthy stalls - standing up. There was not even a place for the animals to sleep. When Pekka was called to account by the veterinarians, his mood changed completely. An acquaintance of his later reported that Seppänen, in a rage, tore all his prizes and awards off the walls and out of the cupboards and destroyed everything. Nothing was left, not even the smallest piece. Seppänen emphasized that now it was all over with! It was part of his former life, he said.

Of the 10-20 cows that were in the barn at the time, several had to be killed by order of the court. The following week, the former cattle farmer is put in custody on suspicion of murder, as police investigations since the spring of 2015 have suggested shocking facts: a total of eight people died on Seppänen's farm and in his summer home in Kontiolahti between 2004 and 2014. In addition, he demonstrably threatened at least 15 people with death.

But luck still seems to be on the farmer's side. His lawyer manages to get him out of pre-trial detention despite the seriousness of the charges. For the Eastern Finnish Court of Appeal makes a fateful decision: In the case of Pekka Seppänen, there was not enough evidence to justify pre-trial detention. He poses no obvious danger. As a result, Seppänen is released at the beginning of 2016.

In fact, it is only the trial at the end of 2016 in the North Karelia District Court that reveals the full extent of his crimes. It is a trial that not only drags the farmer's atrocities into the light of day, but also raises numerous questions with regard to the approach of the law enforcement authorities in North Karelia. Did local police officers possibly let him go for years out of fear for their own safety and integrity? Did they simply want to avoid trouble?

One thing is immediately noticeable at the beginning of the trial: even in court, Seppänen initially manages to let everyone play by his rules again. He consistently disguises himself, as he explains to the judges, in order not to be recognized in public. He is afraid of being exposed to attacks otherwise. The farmer must have presented this so credibly that he is allowed to make himself unrecognizable when the media are present. At the beginning, Seppänen therefore wears a large fur hat, which he pulls deep into his face, as well as an oversized coat with a high collar, in which the corpulent man completely disappears. But this seems to become increasingly uncomfortable in the course of the trial. Therefore, the defendant comes off this and wears only a baseball cap, large sunglasses and a long, black fake beard. However, the true face of the farmer, near whom so many people lost their lives, remains hidden from the public. For the court, it is natural to protect his personal rights.

The long criminal record of Pekka Seppänen also comes up during the trial. Since 2002, he has committed crimes every year without exception. The offenses include, for example, several traffic offenses, bodily harm, threats and animal protection offenses. On several occasions, restraining orders have been issued to protect other people from him.

It is also striking that the farmer repeatedly lends his car to acquaintances who are heavily intoxicated. And from 2004 the strange deaths on his estates and the unfortunate boat trips begin.

A large number of witnesses are questioned, but not all of them dare to testify in Seppänen's presence. At least six litigants and witnesses ask to be allowed to make their statements behind a screen. Even now, they are apparently extremely shy of the defendant. What they all have in common is another peculiarity: each of these intimidated people - without exception! - emphasizes his fear of the great Pekka Seppänen and some of them state that even the police officers who have been on the properties several times over the years have pointed out their fear of him. This, they say, was also the reason for all the retracted statements.

The sad truth of the matter is that a witness who comes from the ranks of the police also prefers to stay behind the privacy screen. He too does not want to expose himself to Seppänen's gaze.

Throughout the statements, the farmer is described as choleric, incredibly long-lasting angry as well as extremely vindictive. He is a person who dominates others, a subjugator, he says.

"This man is a psychopath, a monster!" one witness summarized his feelings in a later interview.

Finally, the verdict in the Pekka Seppänen case is scheduled for January 17. As the man is not in custody but at large even during the entire period of the trial, he is to be picked up as on each of the trial days. But when the police show up at his residence in Jaamankankaantie on the morning of January 17 to take him to court, the officers are in for a nasty surprise. They are faced with an empty, abandoned building. Everything is quiet, no human being is to be seen or heard anywhere. Do they have a bad feeling right away when Seppänen doesn't open the door when they first politely ring the bell? Or do they need a little time to understand? Even when the doorbell rings several times, the door does not open. Knocking is of no use either. Even loud calls and requests to finally come out go unheard. The farmer has left in good time before the verdict is pronounced.

There are indications that Seppänen had help in escaping from his responsibility. His car stands on the yard and was recognizably not used for some time. Apparently, he could count on the support of one of his friends.

Nevertheless, the court decides to pronounce the sentence that day - in the absence of the accused cattle farmer. It is 14.5 years in prison. Seppänen is also sentenced to pay 62,000 USD in damages. In the verdict, he is charged with two murders, aggravated manslaughter, three attempted murders, violation of alcohol laws, assault and pimping.

What irritates one of the trial observers, criminal justice professor Matti Tolvanen, is the fact that neither the purpose of the passive killing nor the boat as a means of committing the crime are discussed in more detail in the trial. Instead, Seppänen is ultimately convicted of negligence. He intentionally caused boats to capsize and did not help the other passengers, even though he knew they were not good swimmers.

Immediately after the verdict is handed down, a full-scale manhunt for Seppänen is launched throughout Finland. In the process, the previous promise by the North Karelia court that he would be allowed to remain anonymous in public is overridden. The image of Pekka Seppänen is all over the media. The man stares from the front pages of almost every daily newspaper. He is a hulking man with a square, beefy skull. His hair is shaved short, and he wears a three-day beard. His features reveal that life has not dealt with him well; alcohol has left its mark.

All over the country people speculate where the serial killer could be. Some think of suicide, others believe in an escape to Russia or even to Southern Europe. But the reality is much more unspectacular. After only three days on the run, Seppänen is caught on January 21 - in nearby Joensuu. There, near the marketplace, he is sitting in a friend's car and is confronted. He has remained close to his crime scenes.

In the following, a tough struggle for the conviction of Pekka Seppänen begins. His lawyer files an appeal against the verdict. There would be weighty reasons that it was a miscarriage of justice. This time the trial takes place before the Court of Appeal of Eastern Finland and the panel rolls up the case even more thoroughly. A psychiatric report on the defendant is ordered and eagerly awaited. The intention now is to finally understand how Seppänen's deeds could have come about. What kind of person is he? What motivates him? Is he himself a severely traumatized person who perhaps cannot fight an overpowering inner urge? The result is sobering. The details of the expert report remain under lock and key, only one fact leaks to the public: Seppänen is fully capable of culpability. He was well aware of the scope of his actions.

After the new insights, the court of appeal confirms the verdict of the first instance. In its reasoning, it emphasizes that this man was "dangerous to the life, health or freedom of others"; for this reason, he must be held accountable for his actions and serve the full prison sentence.

This means the end of any application for early release or parole. Pekka Seppänen can now only be released on parole after his sentence expires in 2030. Until then, the, at that time, 52-year-old will remain in prison. The former cattle farmer does not have to file an extra application for release, but will automatically get out of prison on the first day after fully serving his sentence.

Seppänen is spending the detention in Sukeva Prison on the border between Pohjois-Savo and Kainuu. According to his lawyer, he has adapted quickly to life there.

But the man convicted as a repeated murderer is not yet admitting defeat. In 2018, he has his lawyer file a second-instance motion with Finland's Supreme Court to fight the verdict. The application is rejected. According to his lawyer Seppo Hytönen, Pekka Seppänen is disappointed by the decision.

At the end of 2019, Seppänen's creditors agree to foreclose on his properties in Kontiolahti and Tohmajärvi. He owes victims of his crimes, relatives and others a total of well over 130,000 USD. In addition, further debts of more than 50,000 USD are entered in the enforcement register. As expected, the online auction met with lively interest. A starting bid of 666 euros is set for the small farm, which had not previously appeared as a crime scene. But after a few days, in early 2020, there are already 18 bidders and 21 bids. The price: 30,200 USD. In return, the buyer receives a property with a total of 11.8 hectares, of which more than six hectares of farmland and the rest mainly forest.

To take the shyness away from potential bidders, the sale announcement contains a special clause: the buyer is entitled to official support if Seppänen appears on site after the auction ...

Some witnesses from the first trial also don't want to take any chances. One witness changed his name after the trial, another moved to the US. Moreover, almost no one has dared to say anything publicly about Pekka Seppänen and his deeds by mentioning his name until today.

CHAPTER 3

In the night

(by Marie van den Boom / Mordgeflüster der Podcast)

The calendar reads November 30, 2006, a Thursday. In Ulvila, a small town in western Finland, temperatures are relatively mild for this time of year. Temperatures remain above freezing, only the wind blows quite strongly in between.

At around 9 p.m., Jukka Lahti is on his way home from a business trip that has taken him to Turku, a city a little further away. Normally, the 51-year-old family man has worked for four years as a human resources developer at the local copper plant, which provides the livelihood for many of the families in Ulvila and the surrounding area. And it has done so for generations, as if it were almost a family member itself. For Jukka, the copper mill had been a career move. He moved to

Ulvila from the north with his wife Anneli and four children especially for this job.

Jukka is lost in his thoughts during the car ride. Things are not easy at work at the moment. The company is laying off more than a hundred and fifty employees, and he is one of those who have to break the news to the workers as gently as possible. He's not making any friends with them. He has already had his new Opel Zafira scratched once. But what does that matter. He is not afraid of that.

The closer he gets to Ulvila, the narrower the streets become. The many small single-family houses along the way are hardly distinguishable. Everywhere you see red brick, wooden siding and white-painted window frames. Here and there are trampolines in the front yard, in between a few hideous plastic chairs on the terraces and far too many trimmed hedges.

Then finally Jukka has made it. His family's house appears in front of him. Hardly distinguishable from that of the neighbors. Around 11 p.m., he turns into the driveway and looks forward to seeing his wife, who is surely already expecting him, and the little ones, who are hopefully already lying peacefully in their beds and sleeping.

He gets out, stretches and smooths his dark jacket once more. He's been up since 6 a.m. today, and the car ride has given his suit a few wrinkles and creases. Jukka pays a lot of attention to his appearance. He always appears well-groomed and neatly dressed. His distinctive face, square jaw, full lips and bushy eyebrows stand out. He also has very dark hair.

As Jukka approaches the front door, everything inside the house is already dark. Nothing unusual. In most of the houses in the residential area, there are no lights on at this hour. Jukka opens the front door and, as usual, puts his cell phone on the dresser in the hallway. The doors to the children's rooms are closed, and the little ones are already asleep. Amanda, the oldest daughter, in her own room and the three smaller ones, aged seven, four and two respectively, together in the other. In the hallway he sees their Advent calendars. Tomorrow morning is the day. The children have been looking forward to it for days. Finally, the first door can be opened.

In the fireplace room, his wife Anneli is already in bed. The parents are sleeping there at the moment, as Jukka uses the third room as an office. Next to her lies the youngest daughter. This happens more often. The youngest has great problems to fall asleep and more often still demands the closeness of her mother.

It is very cramped in the room; the red bed sheets should have been changed weeks ago. Since the fourth child has arrived, Anneli can no longer keep up with the household chores.

His pretty partner with the long dark brown hair lies as always on the wall side of the bed. Jukka suffered a serious injury to his leg in a traffic accident when he was young, and since then it has been too burdensome for him to crawl to the wall side every night.

When his youngest daughter catches sight of him, sleep is out of the question. The toddler jumps up and joyfully runs towards Jukka. He hugs her lovingly and then carries her back to Anneli in bed. Afterwards he cleans the dishwasher, which is his job in the household, and brings the little one back to the nursery after she has finally fallen asleep.

Shortly after midnight, Anneli and Jukka fall asleep cuddled together. The whole house is dark and silent.

What happens next is to keep the Finnish authorities on their toes for the next few decades and provides the material for one of Finland's most famous criminal cases.

At 2:43 a.m. sharp on December 1, 2006, the emergency call center receives a call. On the other end, a totally distraught woman's voice is heard. She reports that she and her family urgently need help. An unknown person has broken into her house and stabbed her husband with a knife. He is bleeding. The injured husband calls desperately for help during the phone call. The wife gives the phone to her daughter and rushes to him. The daughter also pleads with the woman at the emergency call center. Rescue workers must come as quickly as possible to help her dad. "Dad, don't die!" she calls out to him.

The phone call ends after four minutes and eighteen seconds, and after another three minutes and twenty seconds, the first officers arrive. What they find is almost unbearable even for the most experienced investigators.

One of them is Juha Joutsenlahti. The 52-year-old, experienced police officer has been working at the police station in the neighboring town for thirty years. Actually, he is currently on vacation and has two more unsolved murders on his hands. But when he sees his colleague's name flicker up on his cell phone, he immediately realizes that his vacation is now over. Complaining is useless.

Cautiously, he enters the crime scene. The glass of the patio door has been smashed, and there are shards of glass on the floor. As soon as the officers enter the fireplace room, they see blood splatter everywhere, some even up to the ceiling. A bloodstained bed sheet lies on the bed, next to it a log with blood on it. The victim lies lifeless next to the bed.

The body can be quickly identified. It is the 51-year-old family man Jukka Lahti. A closer look reveals that his face has been completely smashed. Especially the right side of his face has been hit. His right eye is hanging out of the eye socket. The rest of his body was covered with seventy knife wounds. There is no doubt. Such injuries can only be caused by completely uninhibited and barbaric blows and stabs. Everyone involved is shocked.

On the tiles of the fireplace room, the officers find a bent fillet knife, the tip broken off. However, the second weapon, which according to the injuries was used, cannot be found despite an intensive search, although sniffer dogs have been in action since dawn, searching the residential area and the adjacent woods for it.

During further investigation of the crime scene, it is noticed that someone has stepped on the plastic chair, which is on the terrace. On it they find footprints. In addition, there are small traces of blood on the windowsill, right next to the patio door to the fireplace room.

According to the initial investigation, the officers suspect that a large person broke the window of the terrace door and gained access to the house through it.

Where is the wife, the officer wants to know. But he is put off. She is already on her way to the nearby hospital. She, too, has been critically injured, stabbed twice in the chest.

When Inspector Juha Joutsenlahti first meets the wife of the man who was killed, twelve hours have already passed. It is the afternoon of December 1, 2006, and Joutsenlahti enters the hospital room. He is not sure what to expect right then. In front of him, in the hospital bed, lies a pale and tired-looking woman. Anneli Auer has barely survived the life-threatening stabs to her lungs.

With effort, Anneli describes to the investigator the course of events from her point of view: "No sooner had she and her husband fallen asleep than she noticed, despite the darkness, that someone was in the room and bending over Jukka. This strange person attacked him. Startled and completely taken by surprise, she tried to help her husband, even wrestled with the attacker, but he stabbed her upper body with the knife. It hurt like hell. Immediately she felt the warm blood coming out of the wound. Reflexively, she jumped over a chest next to the bed and fled from the attacker. She dialed the emergency number in the kitchen. Shortly after, her eldest daughter Amanda also joined her and hid together with her mother. When the rescue workers arrived, they found Anneli standing motionless in the living room. A short time later, she collapsed due to her injuries.

The investigator asks Anneli if she remembers the appearance of the unknown assailant. Yes, she remembers the perpetrator. He had rushed toward her again after she turned on the light in the room. He was wearing a hat or a dark hooded jacket and had reddish cheeks. She estimated his age at forty to fifty years and his height at about six feet. What was striking: he did not speak a word the whole time.

The officer wants to know if Jukka had any enemies. Anneli is no longer sure. Hadn't Jukka once talked about a threat? Hadn't the car also been recently scratched? Unfortunately, Jukka dramatized everything all the time, so she could no longer take him seriously when he said something like that.

All in all, Anneli's statements coincide with the recording of the emergency call. Only Anneli, Jukka and the eldest daughter Amanda can be heard on it. When Joutsenlahti leaves, Anneli Auer seems sad. He feels sorry for her. Finally, she asks the investigator if the children can see their father one more time. The investigator refuses and explains to Anneli what her husband's face looks like. After that, she falls silent and cries.

Back at the station, Juha Joutsenlahti wonders who the woman is who was lying there in front of him at the hospital.

Joutsenlahti's investigations reveal that Anneli Auer met and fell in love with her future husband Jukka Lahti in 1996. Both were working at a labor office in Turku at the time. Anneli is 31 years old at the time, has a master's degree in economics and is also in a steady relationship. Jukka is also already married. But that doesn't stop the two from falling in love. Both leave their previous partners and marry a little later. Together they have four children over the next few years.

The couple moves into the house in Ulvila after Jukka takes the promising job at the copper plant there. Meanwhile, Anneli runs the household and looks after the children. She knows a little about baking and runs a website where you can find recipes, gift ideas and decorating suggestions. Under the heading "Crafting Tips," she explains things like how to make a ghost mobile for Halloween. On another website, she gives slimming tips for mothers and proudly presents her weight loss successes in pictures. She uses a third website to fight discrimination against housewives in Finland. With the advertising on the websites, she contributes a little to the household income. This is important to Anneli. She does not want to be "just" the dependent housewife. In addition, through this task she also experiences recognition for the often exhausting and challenging job as a housewife and mother.

Anneli hardly finds any connections in Ulvila. Even with the neighbors, the family doesn't have much to do; as newcomers, they are always somewhat left out. But this is mainly due to the tight-lipped Anneli. The neighbors can't deal with her and so far, no one has thought of inviting her for coffee.

During the investigation, the police receive dozens of tips from the public. These paint a completely different picture of Jukka Lahti. The supposedly popular and professionally successful family man is described as intelligent but driven by aggressive ambition. Therefore, most suspect that possibly his work colleagues are behind the crime. He is said to have downright mocked the fired employees.

But this widens the circle of suspects. Seven hundred men from his colleagues and their relatives give DNA samples. They are compared with foreign blood, which the officials found on a log. According to Anneli, this is what Jukka used to defend himself. At first, it is the most important lead, since the foreign blood cannot be assigned to anyone. However, disappointment soon follows there is no match when comparing the blood with the log. Years later, it is discovered that the blood came from a crime scene investigator who had injured himself on the job.

A neighbor makes an important statement in 2007. He suspects the attack was meant for him, as he works as an acting instructor and had sharply criticized a former theater student for his performance. In his opinion, the student had simply made a mistake in the house.

Juha Joutsenlahti then emails a photo of this student to Anneli Auer, as he does not have the capacity to make the two-hour drive to see her. Anneli replies that it could have been the man. She also points to him in a lineup. As a result, the man is arrested, but released a few days later. No trace from the crime scene could be linked to him.

Public pressure increases. The press got wind of the matter, but the investigators continue to stay in the dark. Nothing really fits together.

They question relatives, acquaintances and friends of the family and look for motives. Infidelity, sex or homosexuality. All these terms come up. A respected investigator from Helsinki also examines Anneli Auer, but comes to the conclusion that she has nothing to do with the matter.

On August 1, 2008, Joutsenlahti has to hand over the case to another investigator from the department. Joutsenlahti actually wanted to transfer the case to the Federal Police, as he simply can't get anywhere with the investigation, but the local police chiefs are anything but in agreement. They are demanding a breakthrough of their own. No matter what the cost.

A year later, Joutsenlahti hears something through the grapevine that catches his complete attention. It's news he can't believe at first: "Auer has confessed to murdering her husband." Joutsenlahti is stunned. After all, he knows the case like no one else, and if one thing is certain for him, it is that Anneli Auer is innocent.

It turns out that the new head of the investigation has set his sights on Anneli Auer early on. He even hires a psychic and doubts the testimony of the grieving widow. For him, it is incomprehensible how the perpetrator should have come through the smashed window. This is at a height of almost one meter and the opening is only 58 x 120 cm. In addition, shards of glass are sticking out.

All attempts with officials have shown that only the most athletic colleagues, and that with many attempts, managed to get inside the house through this opening.

To further verify their suspicions, the investigators tap Anneli Auer's phone and monitor the house. They also urge Anneli to take a lie detector test, which she fails. However, it later turns out that it was given incorrectly and the result may not be used.

The constant interrogations and the little sleep exhaust Anneli and she increasingly gets a bad feeling. It is a doubt that grows in her from interrogation to interrogation: could she really be sure that she had not murdered her husband?

The unrelenting psychological pressure finally causes the wife and mother to buckle. In one of the countless interrogations, she says that she is probably the murderer because there is no other explanation. Investigators evaluate this statement as a confession and celebrate their breakthrough.

Her eldest daughter, Amanda, joins her in one of the interrogation rooms shortly thereafter. She is just 12 years old at this point. Anneli Auer repeats, in front of her daughter, her statement. Amanda cannot believe what she is hearing, she is distraught. Is her memory a lie? Could her mother really be a murderess? But Amanda shakes her head. What her mother is saying can't be true. She cries and tearfully insists that she saw a strange man.

From this moment on, Anneli's chances of being released soon dwindle rapidly. She has been in custody since the confession and is awaiting trial. The trial begins in early summer 2010 in the Satakunta District Court. The prosecutor describes how he believes the crime took place. This narrative differs in large parts from the statements of Anneli Auer and her daughter Amanda.

According to them, Anneli could not sleep on the night in question, from November 30 to December 1, 2006. She lay awake next to her husband in the fireplace room. Finally, she got up, put some cupboards in the kitchen in order and thought. She didn't think Jukka appreciated her enough. He thought her websites were a crank. When her husband came into the kitchen to take his wife back to bed, the conversation escalated and ended in an argument. Eventually, the two went at each other. Auer took a knife from the cabinet above the sink and the argument continued in the fireplace room. The window was broken, according to the prosecution, when Anneli threw a heavy object at Jukka. Amanda woke up from the shouting, but Jukka sent his daughter back to her room and tried to soothe his wife, "Calm down, Annu!" But she had instead stabbed her husband several times with the knife, and he collapsed. Anneli dialed 911 and thought she had killed him. Jukka regained consciousness, however, and she pressed the phone into her daughter Amanda's hand and ran back to her husband in the fireplace room. There she hit him twice on the head with a heavy object. She then ran back to the receiver. After the call, Anneli Auer had taken off her bloody bathrobe and probably hid the murder weapon in the freezer. She then put on a red T-shirt and stabbed herself twice in the chest to make it look as if the perpetrator had wounded her. Police arrived shortly after the 911 call ended. According to police, the soundtrack of the call supports this assumption of what happened, as there is no strange voice on it, nor any running over broken glass, let alone an escape out the window.

Despite attempts by Auer's defense attorney to exonerate his client and point out the countless inconsistencies in the prosecution's story, Anneli Auer is sentenced to life in prison in June 2010. The court concludes that the reviled woman murdered her husband. But this guilty verdict is controversial among the judges, two were convinced of her guilt and one called for an acquittal.

Anneli eventually gets used to prison. Only her children miss her indescribably. Over time, she becomes more and more like an aunt to the children instead of a mother. They miss the daily routine together. The cuddling and comforting. No one calls for her anymore because they have quarreled with their brother or sister.

The children now live with Anneli's brother Ari and his wife. He has made her a solemn promise to always stand by her.

In spring 2011, the appeal hearing begins, in which Anneli recants her testimony. She affirms that she and her husband had never been in conflict and had had a very nice and harmonious relationship overall.

During the trial, something incredible comes to light. Anneli Auer learns that the police had an undercover agent on her for several months. Seppo - yes, she remembers him well. He was the one she dated for a few months in 2009. He had been great with the kids, and they had started falling in love, even wanted to move in together. At least that's what she thought, but by all appearances, she had just been sounded out. What a disgrace. In retrospect, she noticed some inconsistencies. Had Seppo really borrowed the axe one evening to open his jammed door, as he had claimed? Or was it only because he suspected it was the second, missing murder weapon?

Despite the effort, the action has brought investigators neither proof of guilt nor exoneration for Anneli.

Ultimately, the prosecution sticks to its story of the night of the crime. But this time, the appeals court decides unanimously in favor of an acquittal. No sooner is the verdict pronounced than Anneli wants only one thing: to get to her children as quickly as possible. She is so looking forward to the reunion.

But things turn out differently.

Anneli receives a letter from the public prosecutor's office. What she reads in it leaves her speechless. Without understanding, she shakes her head. It is the testimony of her three youngest children. One more absurd than the other. The children told stories of sadism, sexual perversions and cruelty to animals. Anneli's brother had filmed the children doing this and sent these videos to the prosecution.

Amanda is not seen in any of the videos. She is living in a home at this time and no longer with her younger siblings. She felt too confined and controlled with her uncle and his wife. In the fall of 2011, she is picked up by police officers during class. Afterwards, her room and all her belongings are searched, and her computer is confiscated. Amanda is examined by doctors all over her body. They look for cross-shaped cuts, which they say were also found on her siblings. These are supposed to be signs of ritual acts.

Thus, Anneli Auer is arrested again a few weeks after her release. Now on suspicion of child abuse and sexual abuse. The verdict comes in June 2012 and is seven years in prison.

Amanda no longer understands the world, she cries and is beside herself. She has a very intimate relationship with her siblings and simply cannot understand their statements. Shortly after, the eldest daughter is taken to a psychiatrist and even has to spend a week in the closed ward. But that doesn't change anything, she remains steadfast and holds the view that her siblings were influenced by her uncle and aunt. It remains strange that the stories of abuse and Satanism were only suddenly told by the three youngest siblings in 2011, five years after the murder of Jukka Lahti.

The prosecutor now senses his chance. If Anneli Auer really worships the devil, abuses children and tortures animals, then perhaps she was also capable of murdering her husband.

For the press there is no stopping her. Everywhere Anneli is insulted as a Satanist, witch and devil woman with cold blue eyes. It develops into a real hunt.

The public prosecutor's office also continues unperturbed and has the murder trial reopened in 2012. In fact, the first two verdicts are subsequently overturned by the Supreme Court.

Further statements by the younger siblings heavily incriminate both Anneli and Amanda. Amanda's brother Alexander, who was 7 years old at the time of the crime, testifies that his mother and Amanda killed his father together. They would have recorded Jukka's screams and played them back during the 911 call to pretend he was still alive.

Alexander states that he woke up in the night and heard the patio door being opened from his childhood bedroom, as well as the whirring and clicking of the tape recorder.

By means of these statements and some other inconsistencies, the public prosecutor's office increases the pressure on Anneli Auer. A sound expert picks apart the emergency call second by second and analyzes it down to the smallest detail. Everything is laid out against Anneli Auer.

Although the investigator Juha Joutsenlahti even testifies for Anneli Auer at the trial and points out again that there is only some circumstantial evidence but no proof of her guilt, Anneli is again sentenced to life in prison in 2013. It is a very controversial sentence.

The investigator paid a high price with his testimony in court. It costs him his career. He is suspended, but after one and a half years he is allowed to start working for the police again. Only now, instead of investigating murders, he takes care of passports and driver's licenses. When asked if he regrets having testified for Anneli Auer, he answers with a clear no. He would do it again and again.

Anneli also continues to fight and appeals. Even her lawyer now doubts the Finnish legal system.

The legal costs at this point already amount to 1.5 million USD, making this the most expensive trial in Finnish legal history.

In 2015, the appeal proceedings take place in Vaasa. The court doubts the children's testimony and also that Anneli faked the murder attempt. Thus, she is acquitted again. For the second time.

The public prosecutor's office, however, remains stubborn and does not want to be satisfied with an acquittal. It asks for the verdict to be overturned and insists that the Supreme Court must issue a ruling. On the credibility of the judicial system.

Finally, the Supreme Court announces its decision on December 18, 2015, almost 9 years after the death of Jukka Lahti. It remains with the acquittal of Anneli Auer. The latter was released from prison shortly before, having served her sentence for child abuse.

After the acquittal, Anneli is incredibly relieved, she feels a huge weight off her mind. But she still can't really be happy. After this farce, Anneli Auer has lost her faith in justice. She was not only robbed of ten years of her life, no, it was basically completely destroyed.

Anneli is seeking damages. She is asking for several hundred USD for each of the nearly six hundred days she spent in prison. And indeed: in 2016 she receives 545,800 USD in damages for the time she had to spend in prison on suspicion of murder. It is the highest sum ever paid in compensation in Finland.

But all the money in the world can't heal the wounds. Anneli hides behind sunglasses and lives a very secluded life. Everyone in Finland knows her face from the newspapers and the press.

Amanda has tried to contact her younger siblings during and after the trial. However, all attempts were unsuccessful. The siblings do not want to know anything about her. Anneli's efforts to find out about her children's lives were also unsuccessful. She cannot get past the social worker in charge, because the children have forbidden her to give Anneli any information about them and their whereabouts.

The murder of Jukka Lahti is considered the most mysterious criminal case in Finnish history and remains unsolved to this day. But one thing is certain: the murderer has not only the father of the family, but the whole family on his conscience.

CHAPTER 4

The two brothers

His index finger clings ever tighter around the trigger. The grip of the gun lies heavy in his trembling, ice-cold right hand, while he supports the blue-black shimmering barrel with his other hand. The gun feels oily somehow, smells unfamiliar - especially to someone who has never had such a thing in their fingers before. The weight of the gun weighs infinitely heavily in the young man's hands, wanting to pull him to the ground with it; only with difficulty can he resist it and remains standing, swaying slightly. Even though he can only dimly make out the others in the darkness of the night at this moment, he feels their presence so intensely that the tiny hairs on the back of his neck stand up. His breath catches in his throat as he continues to raise the rifle with his leaden, numb arms and holds the muzzle of the rifle barrel almost directly against the back of the person's neck. Only ten centimeters of space are between life and death ... Until, in one fell swoop, the incomprehensible happens.

For the police officers, it is initially a casual routine case when a middle-aged woman shows up at the Oulu police station on November 6, 2018. She is noticeably unsteady as she waits her turn to speak to the police at last. When asked by officers what brings her here, the woman excitedly explains she wants to file a missing person's report. Her older son, 24-year-old Tuomas Heikkinen, had disappeared. She doesn't know where he is and can't reach him by phone. That alone doesn't worry the police officers on duty - a 24-year-old man has his own adult life after all - but the mother is worried for very specific reasons. Both Tuomas and his 20-year-old brother Samuli had struggled with drug problems in the past, and the two of them had attracted attention on several occasions. However, this time it looked as if they had managed to withdraw from drugs. Until Tuomas' disappearance, the two sons lived in a dormitory and supposedly everything had finally gone well. Tuomas even became the father of a baby daughter.

But now, the woman is sure, something bad must have happened! First and foremost, she is massively irritated by the younger brother's behavior. He has repeatedly asked his mother to go to the police - Tuomas' disappearance must be cleared up as quickly as possible. However, when the mother asks what happened, Samuli behaves very strangely. At first, he says nothing, just shakes his head. Then he suddenly mentions the names of two men. Samuli writes the mysterious names on a piece of paper and blankly puts it in an envelope. "If anything happens to Tuomas," he says as he hands the envelope to his mother, "here are the names." With these words, the woman hands the envelope to the baffled officials.

Based on the mother's disturbing account, the Oulu police immediately put Tuomas Heikkinen on the missing persons list and begin searching for him. At first, the matter is considered to be one of the many missing persons cases that clear themselves up after a short time. But it finally dawns on the officers that something can't be quite right here. Even after several weeks of searching, there is no sign of life from the 24-year-old. No one has seen him recently, no one has had any contact with him. It is almost as if the earth had swallowed him whole.

The matter becomes more and more mysterious and finally the police officers have to consider a new, more terrible possibility: Is Tuomas maybe dead?

After all, the young man had been hanging around in the Oulu drug scene for some time and was no stranger to it. Could he have relapsed and not paid for his " stuff"? Had he run up debts with a dealer, or had he run into someone else's car? The more the investigators ask around, the more inconsistencies come to light. Inspector Anti Palokangas takes over the case and starts investigating a possible murder.

Then, in December 2018, a small sensation follows that unleashes an avalanche of events: a total of four young men are arrested. Does this development turn out to be an important piece of the puzzle in the mysterious case surrounding Tuomas

Heikkinen? The police announcement initially only states that the four men committed a murder together and hid the body in a local gravel pit. All four suspects plead not guilty. One of the young men is specifically suspected of alleged murder, two counts of aggravated assault, and aggravated extortion, but the court lets him walk free for the time being.

The investigators are gradually uncovering more and more details about the case. There is growing evidence that the murder took place on the night of October 6 or 7 - in a gravel quarry on the northeastern outskirts of Oulu. Police believe that this must have been a planned crime. Almost as if someone had staged an execution, perhaps even set an example for someone. The victim had been brought to the gravel pit in the Soramontu district, where the murder took place, around 3 a.m. in a dark Audi A6 or a Renault Laguna. Despite an intensive and wide-ranging search of the gravel pit, no trace of the murdered man can be found, so the body was obviously taken away after the crime. There are no clues as to where the body was taken. The suspects remain silent or claim to know nothing. The Jääli gravel pit, known to be a popular crime spot in Oulu due to the lack of surveillance cameras, is located in a hilly and heavily wooded area - perfect for quickly making something disappear that should never reappear.

Palokangas is counting on the good noses of the cadaver-sniffing dogs provided to him by police stations from all over Finland. Up to five dogs are in action every day, but the winter sets clear limits to the search for the murdered man.

Until after the snow melts in the spring, the inspector and his colleagues have no real chance of discovering the dumping ground. Therefore, the police are again urgently asking the people of Oulu for any relevant information. Has anyone perhaps observed anything strange during the night? Who has seen the dark vehicle? Has anyone noticed any unusual noises or people at the Jääli gravel pit?

But the real blow comes when the names of the four young men gradually come to light, shedding a spark of light on the tangled affair: They are Jani Rissanen, Harri Hietamäki, Jimmy Leinonen, and - Samuli Heikkinen! All young men in their twenties who have already committed crimes and are therefore known to the police. But the naming of Samuli Heikkinen is a real shock for all Finns following the story. Tuomas' younger brother, of all people, is suspected of having somehow been involved in the incident. There is a hot debate on the Internet in social networks and also in forums as to what role the 20-year-old may have played. Can it be a coincidence that Samuli, whose brother disappeared without a trace, is now being questioned about a possible murder? Is he in cahoots with the murderers of his supposedly dead brother? Other writers assume that the young man was a kind of "bait" for Hietamäki and Leinonen to lure Tuomas to the crime scene. What happened here? Rumors are circulating, but the most important piece of the puzzle is still missing: the dead man.

In January 2019, one of the suspects is released, it is Jani Rissanen. The young man credibly asserts that he was not present at the crime. He had only lent his car to the others on the evening in question and had nothing more to do with the whole affair. The other men continue to be questioned intensively. Finally, the house of cards collapses. The suspects admit that someone did indeed die in the gravel pit, but they all deny intent. And then something else comes to light that brings the decisive turn in the case.

When the snow and ice have thawed, the search for the body is resumed and finally the decisive breakthrough is made. On May 7, 2019, the task forces discover the body of a man: it is indeed Tuomas Heikkinen. Thus, the fate of the disappeared is now a sad certainty.

During questioning, Hietamäki, the nephew of a two-time murderer, and Leinonen confess to having hidden the body in a large black bag weighted down with chains in a wooded area just a few kilometers away. More precisely, they sank the bag in a drainage pond and then, as a precaution, weighed it down with stones so that it could not rise to the surface under any circumstances. Then, in one of the following nights, they went back to Jääli and removed their traces as best they could. The find confirmed what they had said.

The widely anticipated trial in Oulu District Court is scheduled for Midsummer Week. June 17 marks the start of one of the most dramatic trials in Finnish criminal history.

Even the prelude to the mysterious gravel pit murder is a sensation. A total of seventeen criminal offenses are to be tried on that day, and seven young men from Oulu are accused. In addition to drug offenses, there are serious violations of domestic peace, deprivation of freedom in a particularly serious case, violations of the peace of the dead, firearms offenses and several more. Three of the men are accused of the murder of Tuomas Heikkinen: besides Harri Henriek Hietamäki and Jimmy Johannes Leinonen, Tuomas' little brother Samuli is also accused. The whole of Finland is waiting in suspense to see if the biblical story of Cain and Abel has indeed been repeated here. Was it fratricide?

Because the main hall of the Ratakatu courthouse is not large enough to accommodate all the people involved, guards, a police unit and the curious spectators, another hall is added for the proceedings without much ado. In this room, the trial can be followed by video. The proceedings are scheduled to last a total of four days, with the day of the verdict not yet scheduled. Furthermore, the individual offenses are to be dealt with on different days; Wednesday and Thursday are planned for the murder case.

The main courtroom offers an unusual sight on these memorable days: A large privacy screen divides it into two sections, so not all defendants can see each other. The three men accused of murder are seated in the front area, while the seats behind the screen are reserved for those on trial for lesser offenses related to the murder case.

The trial gets off to a somewhat chaotic start: for example, two of those summoned to appear do not show up at all, and another is late. Hietamäki, Leinonen and Heikkinen cover their faces as the media are allowed into the courtroom and filming begins. But those who catch a glimpse are surprised and horrified at the same time. All three still look like children, especially the blond Samuli with his roundish face looks more like a little rascal. Can someone like that be capable of killing his own brother, even executing him in cold blood?

The slender Hietamäki also looks more like a teenager, despite his slicked-back blond hair, his thin three-day beard and the mustache fuzz. Leinonen, on the other hand, is a much more compact guy with a bull neck. His dark hair stands up in a tousled fashion, an attempt at a particularly cool, modern hairstyle.

In his opening statement, the prosecutor demands that the three defendants be sentenced to long prison terms. He considers it proven that they killed Tuomas Heikkinen in full consciousness and in a particularly brutal and cruel manner in the Jääli gravel pit. In his statements he even compares the act with a regular execution. He therefore clearly demands: a life sentence.

While up to this point the public had to rely on speculation and snippets of information, what exactly happened on the night of October 6-7 in Oulu is now becoming known in concrete terms for the first time. The court recapitulates the events as follows.

Tuomas and Samuli had once again gotten into trouble for drugs, the prosecution reports. This time it was amphetamine worth about 2,000 USD, which had apparently disappeared without a trace. Whether the two Heikkinen brothers embezzled it or simply couldn't pay their debts to Hietamäki and Leinonen, the dealers, is unclear. The fact is, this time the two brothers had fallen in with the wrong people.

On the evening of October 6, Tuomas and Samuli were partying with a friend and at least one other acquaintance in their apartment in Tuira. Although it is only between 6 and 7 p.m. on this Saturday night, they are already drinking. The young woman, who is just 19 years old, has known both brothers for some time. With one of them she went to elementary school together, with the other she even had a relationship for a short time. The woman told the police that Tuomas had always been in debt to someone as long as she had known him.

Sometime that evening, the doorbell rings. It is three men in their mid-twenties, whom the 19-year-old does not know. Since they explain that they want to visit the brothers, the young woman takes the strange visitors upstairs to the apartment.

When two of the men enter the living room where the two brothers had just made themselves comfortable on the couch, Samuli and Tuomas turn white as a sheet. They immediately recognize Hietamäki and Leinonen. Assuming that the two dealers are friends of the brothers, the 19-year-old retreats to the kitchen with her acquaintance and the third man - an alleged buyer of the missing drugs.

When she returns to the living room a short time later, she is confronted with a surprising scene: Both brothers are standing there stark naked. Completely taken aback, the meanwhile heavily drunk woman asks what is going on here. As an answer she only receives the saying: This is nothing for girls' eyes ...

But even from the next room, the 19-year-old hears that the two brothers are being beaten up by the "guests" in the worst possible way. First Tuomas and Samuli get slaps in the face, later the toilet lid is hit on their heads. When one of the brothers staggers into the kitchen to wash the blood off his face, he begs for help. The situation is extremely frightening and scary, as the witnesses later state, the brothers must be going through unbelievable fears. "I have never seen anyone so afraid," they say in court. In contrast, Hietamäki and Leinonen spread a completely different mood. Both appear in the best of moods, appear extremely dominant and determined. And they are ready to bargain for a man's life.

Hietamäki's account of what happened in the living room makes your blood run cold. The treatment of the two still naked young men borders on torture. While they stand there trembling and completely terrified, Hietamäki and Leinonen resort to exceedingly radical and morbid means in their questioning about the missing drugs. They inform the brothers that one of them will die unless they reveal where the amphetamine is. To determine whom it will hit, the two dealers play rock-paper-scissors. Without further ado, they line up in front of each other, one standing for the older brother, and the other for the younger one with the bigger debt to the dealer duo.

"Rock, Paper,....!"

It all becomes too much for Samuli. He is so scared for his life that he panics and agrees to kill his older brother if it means he will escape with his own life! However, he still cannot or will not reveal where the drugs are.

Suddenly everything goes very fast. The four men, the two Heikkinens as well as Hietamäki and Leinonen, leave the apartment in Tuira. The people in the kitchen can still see how Samuli is completely distraught. Then the four of them all enter a dark Audi A6 in front of the house.

They drive through Oulu at night. The destination is the Jääli gravel pit in Soramontu, which is both very remote and very extensive. Moreover, there are no cameras installed to monitor the area. Those who come here are guaranteed peace and quiet.

On site, the Heikkinen brothers have to get out of the car, one of the dealers threatens them with a gun so that they don't do anything stupid. Tuomas is forced to stand on the edge of a pit, while Samuli is handed a gun. Cynically, they demand that the younger brother make good on his promise from the apartment now. He should shoot Tuomas right here and now

- otherwise they would both die. The two dealers emphatically underline their threat with the weapons they hold in their hands.

The two brothers are faced with the most agonizing minutes of their lives. Samuli, who is under drugs, stress and alcohol, is faced with the decision of who should die. Tuomas, who waits on the edge of the pit while his life is bargained for behind his back. And then the fate seems sealed: Samuli actually raises the rifle and points the barrel at his brother's neck. He pulls the trigger.

A clicking sound is heard - but no shot is fired!

There is no cartridge in the barrel. Does any hope sprout in the brothers - was this all just some kind of morbid test? Hietamäki explains that it was indeed a test. He wanted to make sure that Samuli would actually follow through with what he promised in Tuira. Now the 25-year-old loads the gun, hands it back to Samuli and orders him to shoot. At this, the dealers point their gun at the younger Heikkinen and again, Samuli obeys. For the second time, he points the barrel of the gun at his brother, who is standing on the precipice with his back to him, waiting for the unimaginable. Only ten centimeters lie between the muzzle of the gun barrel and Tuomas' neck.

Then a shot shatters the silence of the night. Tuomas is dead on the spot. Executed by his own little brother.

Samuli drops the rifle and staggers into the night, but Hietamäki and Leinonen pick him up again and then take him back to Tuira. To the apartment where the terrible events of that night had begun.

Samuli does not tell his friends about what happened in Soramontu. He also does not reveal where his brother has gone. To his acquaintance, the young man only mentions that she should not tell anyone about what happened that night. He is terrified of Hietamäki and Leinonen, but he cannot tell the police anything. After all, he knew what the dealers would do to him then. Besides, if something came out, he would be the only one who could be held responsible ...

In early July, the verdict is announced by the Oulu District Court. Hietamäki is sentenced to 9 ½ years in prison for incitement to manslaughter and for other minor crimes. Leinonen, who has repeatedly claimed that he was only present at the scene but never actively involved in the murder of Tuomas, is sentenced to 10 years and 2 months. He is charged with incitement to manslaughter and two counts of aggravated deprivation of liberty. Because he took Tuomas' body from Jääli to the forest to dump it in the drainage pond, he also committed a disturbance of the peace of the dead.

But the verdict in the case of Samuli Heikkinen caused a real stir. He had repeatedly claimed that he shot his older brother in self-defense. Otherwise, he himself or even both of them would have been killed. Samuli is sentenced to five years in prison, for the court has proven that he committed manslaughter - albeit under conditions resembling duress. However, a situation of self-defense in the legal sense had not existed. For this, Samuli's life would have had to be more valuable than that of his older brother. The judge went on to explain that one cannot sacrifice a life in order to save another.

Many people felt sorry for the childlike Samuli Heikkinen after the decision was announced; it was difficult for them to follow the court's reasoning. Again and again the question arises whether the killing might not have been some kind of extraordinary emergency. The thought of killing one's own brother is simply inconceivable for quite a few trial observers.

In addition, another question arises: Given the brevity of the trial, were all the important facts perhaps not explored in depth? Were there possibly points that, if examined more closely, would have shed a different light on the facts of the case?

What follows is unsurprising in this respect: Heikkinen, Hietamäki and Leinonen are all appealing the verdict.

The trial before the Rovaniemi Court of Appeal started at the end of February 2020. What is strangely reminiscent of the first trial is the fact that a privacy screen is also being installed here. This time, however, it separates the unlucky shot Samuli Heikkinen from Hietamäki and Leinonen.

Presumably, the prosecutor's motion comes as a real surprise to those present, as he revisits the original motion from the first trial and again demands life imprisonment for Hietamäki and Leinonen.

In his appeal, Samuli Heikkinen insists that he was forced to shoot his brother. This was not sufficiently appreciated by the court at the time. Hietamäki, on the other hand, insists that Samuli made the decision to shoot Tuomas all by himself. It is true that he and Leinonen drove the two brothers to the gravel pit, but this was only done to scare them. A killing was not planned at any time, he says, and he was completely shocked when Heikkinen actually pulled the trigger.

Leinonen, on the other hand, claims in his complaint that he was in no way involved in the incident. Rather, he says, he assumed that Hietamäki had given Samuli an unloaded gun. The fact that the latter had loaded the gun at some point in between completely escaped him. Just being on the scene does not automatically mean being complicit in a murder, Leinonen's lawyer emphasizes.

Moreover, another point is raised this time that hardly played a role in the first trial. According to Hietamäki and also Leinonen, Samuli Heikkinen's testimony is not reliable. On the one hand, he had changed it several times and in this respect contradicted himself, on the other hand, the two brothers had argued violently and even fought with each other before leaving the apartment in Tuira. Maybe that was why Heikkinen had decided to get rid of his older brother?

Once again, the entire case is reopened, but this time with a closer look at the relationship between the four young men. First, the mother of the two Heikkinens is called to the witness stand. Her account of the brothers' lives is moving, as it is the story of two drug addicts who get deeper and deeper into Oulu's very active drug scene and come into contact with people they are no match for. Both brothers had gotten into debt in the scene and got into trouble as a result. In 2018, a man to whom they could not repay a large sum even kept them in his apartment against their will for a while. At that time, the mother received an alarming message from Tuomas, saying, "Mom, I'm so terribly scared, I don't want to die!" As a result, she had alerted the police, who freed the brothers from the situation.

Following this, Tuomas and Samuli did not dare to leave their dormitory for quite a while. Their mother brought them food several times so that they would not have to go out the door.

Samuli did not tell her about Tuomas' death at first, the mother also explained when asked. Although they saw each other several times during that time. Instead, the younger son just kept asking her to report Tuomas missing. On one day Samuli was particularly anxious. That was the day he wrote down the names of the other two defendants and gave her the envelope with his worrying words. She immediately went to the police.

The mother only found out how everything really happened and by whose hand her eldest child died when her youngest son had already been arrested.

After the mother's testimony, Samuli Heikkinen is called. He is visibly agitated and his voice trembles repeatedly. He cannot hold back his tears when he speaks. Once again, he details what happened in the apartment in Tuira: Hietamäki and Leinonen came to the apartment in search of a missing drug package. The two men did not believe the Heikkinens' protestations of innocence. During the brothers' abuse, Hietamäki hit Tuomas in the face with his rifle and asked if someone had to die before the truth could come out.

That was the moment, Samuli reports, when his big brother suddenly said that the dealers should kill the one with the higher debt. That was him, Samuli. Because he was so horrified by this, he cursed at his brother, and an argument ensued.

Finally, the brothers were taken to the car. Before they left, Hietamäki held the rifle in front of them and told them not to be heroes. Samuli explains that the threat had been acted upon. During the entire drive to Soramontu, the two intimidated young men didn't make another sound. When they finally arrived at the Jääli gravel pit, the thought flashed through Samuli's mind: "Things never go well in a place like this ..." But he had no idea at that point how right he was to be.

The following events are also discussed in more detail this time. So Hietamäki had first looked for a suitable place in the gravel pit where Tuomas had to stand. Then he demanded from Samuli that he should shoot now and pressed the rifle directly into his hand. But not without giving him some "well-meant advice" along the way: Hietamäki explained to the younger brother that Tuomas would be dead on the spot if Samuli shot him directly in the neck.

The tears streaming down his face show how much the memory upsets the young man. But he continues, describing how he went to Tuomas and asked him to look at him. One last time they embraced each other and Samuli desperately said: "I have no other choice! I hope you understand!" To which Tuomas replied, "Yes, I understand ..." Then they both still said to each other, "I love you."

Under the gaze of the two 25-year-olds, Samuli then asked his older brother to turn around. It is impossible for him to even look Tuomas in the face with what is about to follow.

With fingers trembling, he pulls the trigger - but Tuomas continues to stand. He does not fall to the ground.

In front of everyone, Hietamäki now loads the rifle with a single cartridge and hands it back to Samuli. All the time Leinonen stands in the background with a loaded gun to make it clear that there is no way out.

And Samuli doesn't refuse. Both brothers know this time the gun is loaded. He pulls the trigger again - and this time Tuomas slumps down.

Samuli presses the rifle into Hietamäki's hand before running off into the night in shock.

It is a moving confession from which those present have to recover for a moment. Heikkinen, too, is still crying. But is his account of what happened that night accurate?

Now Hietamäki and Leinonen have the opportunity to recount their view of what happened on the night of October 6-7, 2018. What they say puts the events in a completely different light. Thus, they emphasize in unison that they had undertaken the trip to the gravel pit only to scare the brothers. With a few blows, the truth about the whereabouts of the drugs should be elicited from them there. In addition, Leinonen claims that he had absolutely nothing to do with the death of Tuomas Heikkinen. It was only out of sheer stupidity that he allowed himself to be persuaded to help remove the body.

Probably in order to make him appear credible, his defense attorney asks a question at this point: whether he, Jimmy Leinonen, was prepared to assault someone? The answer comes promptly: "Yes, always. But that's completely different from murder."

Regarding the weapons that were present at the scene, the version of the two dealers also differs. They would have had only one weapon with them, that of Hietamäki. Because they had overheard the two brothers' argument about the debt matter, they gave Samuli that gun and allowed him to fire a warning shot at his brother. The two 25-year-olds had assumed that he would aim at a leg or a foot; but at no time had they wanted to test whether Samuli would kill Tuomas. On the contrary, they were completely horrified when the younger brother placed the gun barrel in Tuomas' neck and actually pulled the trigger!

For Leinonen, the matter had been even more shocking, after all, he had assumed that Hietamäki's gun was not loaded. That's why he didn't even think about it when he recommended Samuli to shoot at one of Tuomas' legs or feet to teach him a lesson. At first, the dealer didn't understand why the older brother suddenly went down. Then Leinonen understood and asked Samuli why he had done that? Why didn't he shoot at one foot or just miss? In reply he received a terse: it was better that way ...

Hietamäki then describes to the court how Samuli even shouted at him because he wanted his gun so badly. Tuomas should definitely get a lesson from him that evening. Hietamäki then gave him the gun, but according to his own statement, he would never have suspected that Samuli Heikkinen would shoot his older brother in return. This completely shocked Hietamäki. It happened so fast, Hietamäki emphasizes, he did not even see Samuli aiming ...

Does this account correspond to the facts that took place in the Jääli gravel pit that October night? If so, then in truth Samuli would simply be a vengeful fratricide. Someone who, without hesitation, seizes the next best opportunity to get rid of his troublesome brother. At this point, it's testimony against testimony.

The highly anticipated verdict of the Court of Appeals is finally handed down on April 22, 2020, with numerous media representatives on hand to watch the announcement live and record the reactions of the young defendants. The entire public is still captivated by one question: Is Samuli Heikkinen, now 21 years old, the cheerful young man with the rascal grin on his child's face, really a murderer? Is there a kind of modern Cain hiding behind the so harmless-naïve façade, who does not even hesitate to commit such a terrible crime against his closest relative?

When the verdict is finally read out, dead silence reigns in the courtroom. Everyone listens intently to what is said.

The judges in Rovaniemi have decided to partially change the first-instance verdicts. In the opinion of the court of appeal, the case in question is not one of manslaughter but one of murder. The sentence passed against Samuli Heikkinen remains in force. However, Harri Hietamäki's and Jimmy Leinonen's sentences are changed. Hietamäki receives life in prison for incitement to murder and other lesser offenses. In contrast, Leinonen's sentence is reduced; his sentence is now 9 years and 9 months imprisonment for accessory to murder.

The court's decision is a real sensation, especially for all the trial observers who were convinced of Samuli's innocence. Everyone is now all the more eager to hear the judges' reasons for the verdict.

These commence in respect of the offences committed by Harri Hietamäki. For the judges it is clear that his account of events cannot be true. Rather, the death of a brother would have already been a done deal when the two dealers came to the apartment in Tuira. Hietamäki had assaulted Tuomas Heikkinen in the apartment and then a draw had been made to decide which of the two Heikkinens should die. The rock-paper-scissors game is a clear indication that the murder was already decided at this point. Moreover, Hietamäki had arranged everything in the gravel pit in such a way that the affair looked like an execution. The events in the gravel pit were intended to finally solve the problems with the two brothers and at the same time to signal to others that it was better not to mess with Hietamäki and Leinonen.

Even though the versions of the three defendants differ significantly, one thing is a fact for the judges: Hietamäki unlocked his gun and gave it to Samuli. Moreover, Hietamäki had talked Samuli into actually pulling the trigger and even gave tips on how to kill him. Because the younger Heikkinen was on drugs at the time and had been severely intimidated by the previous attacks, he was in a virtually defenseless state, according to the sentencing memorandum. In combination with the execution scene, it must have been clear to all involved: Samuli Heikkinen would kill his brother. This was exactly what Hietamäki had worked towards in a single-minded and extremely cold-blooded manner - and therefore murder had to be assumed in his case.

Jimmy Leinonen is seen as a willing helper of Hietamäki. He himself admitted in court that he was not afraid to use violence when in doubt - and that's exactly what he had made clear that evening, when he attacked the brothers back at the apartment in Tuira and intimidated them in the gravel pit. In the apartment, moreover, he discussed directly with Hietamäki in front of the brothers which of the two was to be shot that evening - so it is not very credible when Leinonen says that it surprised him when Hietamäki put the gun in Samuli's hand. Furthermore, the court is sure that Leinonen must have seen Hietamäki load the gun - and thus he was fully aware of what was about to happen. Although he only played the role of a helper in the whole cruel game in the gravel pit, what Leinonen did on the night of October 7, he did intentionally and in full awareness of the consequences.

With regard to Samuli Heikkinen's verdict, the judges in Rovaniemi are rather brief. They, too, are aware that the circumstances on that fateful evening were truly exceptional. They acknowledge that Samuli was extremely intimidated and also not fully in control of his senses due to the drugs. Nevertheless, Samuli took the gun and ended the life of his brother Tuomas. Without anyone holding his hand in the process. Because in the end, Samuli felt his own life was more valuable than Tuomas'. And that is exactly why the appeal judges see no reason to reduce his sentence.

Following the pronouncement of the verdict, all three convicts, Harri Hietamäki, Jimmy Leinonen and Samuli Heikkinen, are taken away and have to start their prison sentences directly. It is not yet known whether any of them will also appeal against this verdict.

In the meantime, the public discussion about whether the punishment for Samuli Heikkinen is really justified has also died down and the incident has been pushed out of the headlines. For the mother of the two brothers, however, the story will never end. She ultimately lost both sons in her own way.

CHAPTER 5

The sleeping preacher

(By Fabian Maysenhölder/ Secta Podcast)

The day he will have to fight for his life begins at a very relaxed pace for Ernst Venelius. It's a cold January day in 1924, but that's no reason for a true Finn not to take a motorboat out for a spin off the coast of the western Finnish town of Kokkola. Ernst Venelius, a young, strong man with striking facial features, is looking forward to a beautiful day with his sister and father. Both accompany him on this early morning boat trip. A well-deserved time out with the family from his work at the police department.

The clear waters of the Baltic Sea gleam in the winter sun, which rose above the horizon less than an hour ago. In these latitudes, the sun rises late in January, and winters are characterized by long darkness. But that's exactly why Venelius loves this time of day so much: The "Golden Hour" creates a special, diffuse light shortly after sunrise. A magical morning atmosphere that the policeman enjoys - here he is in his element. Here he feels at one with nature. The sea foam surrounds the small boat. He closes his eyes, feels the frothy droplets reaching his face as the boat sails along the coast. It is just before 10 o'clock in the morning.

The young man opens his eyes again and lets his gaze roam over the sun-drenched coast. He takes a deep breath, feeling the cold winter air in his lungs as the sun's rays warm his face. Suddenly, a biting pain runs through him. Only then does the sound of the shot that hit him reach his ear. He is abruptly jolted out of his thoughts. What is happening? His father and sister are screaming loudly. Suddenly he sees his sister topple over to the side. The investigator can no longer grasp a clear thought, staggers forward into the boat. The shooting doesn't stop. The three duck into the small boat as best they can. Ernst sees the blood from his sister's wound before he feels more bullets pierce the thin wood of the boat and hit his body. Before Ernst Venelius falls unconscious after the fourth hit, he hears his father screaming for help.

The story of Maria Åkerblom begins like that of an ordinary girl at that time in Finland. She is born on September 14, 1898, in southern Finland, in a small community called Snappertuna. The family is poor, and Maria is one of nine children. For long periods of time, Maria also lives with her uncle, who lives in the nearby town of Tamisaari.

At an early age, Maria has to take up a job. It is not unusual at that time for young women to be hired as housekeepers - which is what Maria does. Her youth is marked by working as a maid. "Normal, but a little unpredictable and wild" - these are words used by an employer to describe the young Maria. It becomes clear early on that Maria is a young woman who demands a lot of attention and care. Even at an early age, she demonstrates her talent for convincing others of her worth and getting them to do what she wants.

It is not unusual for religion to play a major role for people at that time. Finland is no exception at the turn of the century. Both Maria's family and her changing employers are evangelical Lutherans. Faith plays an important role in everyday life.

At the age of 18, Maria falls seriously ill. So badly that she returns home to her parents. Apparently, her health is deteriorating so much that her mother already invites the family's neighbors to say goodbye. The situation is dramatic. Maria is trembling all over and at times only lives in a state close to unconsciousness. Then, in February 1917, something happens that will significantly shape the rest of her life: Mary becomes a prophetess.

One guest after another crosses the Åkerbloms' threshold to see their dying daughter one last time. Prayers are said. No one knows what will happen to the young girl. There she lies, for weeks. Sick, pale and trembling. She has not spoken a word for days, and even if she did, what she says can hardly be understood. One of the guests holding Maria's hand suddenly feels something. The young woman's body goes ice cold. She stops shivering. She lies there as if dead. Is it over now?

No. Maria is still breathing. She is unconscious.

Then she suddenly opens her eyes and starts talking. Everyone understands her. It is not incoherent talk - Mary speaks of having received messages from God. The young maid is not completely conscious. As if in a trance, she speaks of divine revelations. At the end of her sermon, she tells those present when she will preach next.

With this event Maria Åkerblom is part of a phenomenon called "sleep preachers": People who preach in a state of trance. They are not the kind of sermons you hear in churches up and down the country these days. Due to the special circumstances of apparent unconsciousness, the sermons of sleep preachers are considered by themselves and by their listeners as direct divine revelation. Although there is some evidence of male sleep preachers in the U.S., this phenomenon remains largely confined to Scandinavia and to the 19th and early 20th centuries. And indeed, in Scandinavia it is almost without exception women who are sleep preachers. It is impossible to say today whether the young Mary knew about this phenomenon. But as there were already known sleep preachers traveling around Finland before her, it can be assumed that she had heard about it.

The event described is the birth of a religious movement that will form around Maria's preaching and cause an uproar throughout Finland. Word quickly spreads about what has happened in the Åkerbloms' house. More and more people gather; from time to time, followers of other sleep preachers join in and join Maria. Everyone wants to hear her sermons and revelations. Soon Maria begins to give her sermons in churches as well - framed by liturgical elements. Thus, what the young woman speaks is even given an ecclesiastical authority: Usually, the priest thereby introduces the service, then they sing together, and finally Mary enters the chancel to proclaim her revelations.

Although many attend the services, outsiders are often skeptical of what Mary is doing. One such skeptic is her own brother. He is firmly convinced that Maria is suffering from a mental illness - for a short time, she is therefore admitted to a private psychiatric institution. However, she is not there for long. After her release, she heads for Helsinki. There, in the metropolitan area, she begins to preach.

The year 1919 brings a special relationship for Maria, who is just 20 years old. A wealthy man who would become her most devoted follower enters her life: Forester Eino Vartiovaara. Together with his wife, he comes to one of Åkerblom's trance sessions to listen to her. The two are amazed by what Maria is doing. The couple decides to make their own house available for Maria's trance sessions in the future. A short time later Eino Vartiovaara gives up his profession to devote himself fully to Maria and her movement. That same year, Maria announces a vision that she claims to have received directly from God: The Vartiovaaras, she explained, had been commanded by God to take in a 20-year-old woman as a foster child - the age of majority at that time in Finland was not until the age of 21. That Maria is just 20 years old at this time is certainly no coincidence. Although the forester and his wife already have three biological daughters, they are persuaded on the basis of divine revelation and accept Maria as their foster child.

From then on, people start talking and spreading rumors. Why do the Vartiovaaras take an almost adult daughter as a foster child? What's the point? What is happening in the house is viewed with unease by many. Still, the stream of visitors who come to the trance sessions is uninterrupted. But many of them come out of pure curiosity. The movement around Maria Åkerblom hardly gains any new followers at this time. A short time later, Maria finally convinces her new family to move to Kokkola, a small town on the west coast of Finland.

For Maria, the overall situation is a stroke of luck. By joining her new family, she is no longer poor, but wealthy. She is no longer a maid but has some of her own. She also no longer has to work. She can do whatever she wants all day long. Thus, the young prophetess fully concentrates on her activity as a sleep preacher. In Kokkola, this brings the breakthrough. There she is so successful that at times between 600 and 700 people gather around her. She now holds her trance sessions standing up - no longer lying down, as she did at the beginning. Therefore, she also needs active support during her performances, because she can fall into a trance at any moment. During the services, she often collapses out of nowhere and falls over. Therefore, there are always one or two men behind her to catch her - her foster father Eino Vartiovaara is almost always one of them.

Maria is getting stranger and stranger. The rumors that were already circulating in Helsinki are not made up out of thin air. Things are brewing in the Vartiovaara family. Maria demands more and more: she suddenly wants to sleep in her foster parents' bedroom and demands that her foster mother teach her about sex.

Vartiovaara's wife also becomes more and more suspicious. The wife has to realize that her husband is completely obedient to Maria. Therefore, she even tries to hire a trustee to manage her husband's affairs. Without success. Finally, she sees no other option but to leave. She takes the children and leaves her husband and Maria. But because she can't find a place to go, she returns shortly after. From then on, she leads a life like a prisoner in her own house: Maria's followers torment her psychologically and also physically. Someone is always with her to guard her. Contact with her children is also strictly regulated.

The people are fascinated by the charismatic Maria Åkerblom. A woman with a special talent: she can talk well. Her sermons, with which she captivates her listeners, sound almost poetic. This is precisely a gift that predestines her to be the leader of a new religious movement. When she takes the floor, the crowd almost falls into a kind of "flow state" in which they completely forget their surroundings and time, so fascinated are they by what Maria is telling them. Little by little, Maria takes advantage of this and establishes different "levels" of followers in the Åkerblom movement, which she strictly separates.

From then on, Maria does not only preach to large audiences - often on the grounds that there is someone among them who is critical of her and questions her as well as her teachings. The full access to her and the fullness of her revelations is only given to a small inner circle, which consists of her most loyal followers. The path to reach this innermost level is hard and long. There Mary gathers her most loyal followers. Here, they blindly believe her every word. And everyone in this circle must also take an oath, with which they swear on their lives never to betray the leader.

At the same time, a new house for Maria was being built in Kokkola. The money, labor and wood for it are being procured by her followers. "Maria's Palace", as the building is called, has 2 floors and 19 rooms. Since the building is completely covered in tar, it is also called "Tar Palace" by some. At the time, this was a common practice to protect the wood from moisture.

It soon becomes apparent that the close-knit community around Mary is anything but unproblematic. Not much is known about what goes on there. However, individual court cases and investigations allow a glimpse behind the scenes now and then.

In 1919, Maria and her foster father Eino Vartiovaara are put on trial. They are accused of physically abusing a stable boy. They were sentenced; the penalty can no longer be traced today. But one thing is known: When they leave the building after the trial, they are met by a wild, shouting mob of demonstrators. The former forester and his foster daughter are insulted and abused.

Events like these are snapshots of what is going on in the community: psychological and also physical violence are everyday occurrences in the group. Maria and Eino do not tolerate dissenters and critics. Everyone has to loyally obey what the leadership says. Otherwise, the punishment follows on its heels. No means are spared to make the believers dependent and obedient.

All these events fit together like puzzle pieces in Maria Åkerblom's increasingly sectarian worldview: "them out there" versus "us true believers". Confrontations like the one in front of the courthouse occur more and more frequently - they are a product of the environment's increasingly skeptical attitude towards Maria and her movement. She herself and her followers are convinced: they are being persecuted for the sake of their faith. Thus, the group increasingly isolates itself from the outside world - ordered by Mary herself.

What is the strange relationship between Maria and her foster father all about? What happens at these secret meetings that Maria holds for her inner circle? Why does Maria suddenly start scheduling nightly meetings - and mostly with male visitors? These are just a few of the questions that outsiders have at this time. Questions to which there is still no answer today. Many were therefore very critical and skeptical of the group around Mary even then.

For the new religious movement around the sleeping prophetess, the approaching end of the world is certain. The Åkerblom movement gradually prepares for the apocalypse. Mary herself is not only credited by her followers with receiving prophetic messages from God - the ability to perform (healing) miracles is also associated with her. Mary, her followers believe, has special access to God and also receives indications from God about events not mentioned in the Bible.

Finally, in 1922, something happens that heralds the beginning of the end.

Maria is walking with her large black dog on a path near Kokkola. She often goes out into nature with her dogs. On this day, she encounters a farmer named France Honka, who comes towards her on a horse. Honka knows his horse: he knows that it shies away from dogs, having already been bitten by one.

So Honka tries to keep the dog away from the horse. When Maria passes the farmer on horseback with her animal, he hints at throwing a rock at the dog. When Maria notices this, she blows a fuse: Out of nowhere, she pulls out a gun and shoots the horse. Apparently, everyone is in such a state of agitation that the shot misses its target - no one, not even an animal, is hurt.

Even though this scene ends smoothly, it sets a ball rolling that can no longer be stopped. Honka refrains from bringing charges against Maria after this event. Nevertheless, the young "prophetess" is put on trial. The reason for this is a police officer named Ernst Venelius, who relentlessly pursues the incident. The trial was to become a farce: 20 witnesses swear under oath that it was not Maria but the farmer who fired the shots. They had, they claim, been picking berries in a nearby field and had witnessed the scene. All of them are supporters of Maria.

Venelius is skeptical, from the beginning the whole thing seems strange to him. So, he investigates further and is finally able to prove that most of these alleged witnesses had been several kilometers away at the time in question. They were obviously thoroughly instructed on what to say in court. Some of the perjurers are therefore arrested for giving false testimony under oath. All, however, stick to their version of the story. A dead end for the young investigator.

Nevertheless, the public pressure and hostility that Maria Åkerblom and her movement face intensifies. Thus, a short time later, Maria begins to speak in her prophecies that the city of Kokkola will soon perish - and that the chosen ones must emigrate. Their noble goal: Palestine, the promised land.

So many followers sell their belongings and donate them to the movement. In the spring of 1923, Maria and her most faithful followers, about 220 people, marched off. Away from Kokkola, towards the south. But they do not make it to Palestine. Already in Helsinki they get stranded. With the proceeds of the sales, they are able to buy a property for the group there.

Even though it is generally easier for the group in a big city like Helsinki, Maria's criminal streak increasingly gets to her. The prophetess has to go to prison: she is arrested for stealing fabrics for clothes. Some of her followers are also convicted for repeatedly committing thefts. As they affirm to the police, they were acting on behalf of their "prophetess". They therefore have no sense of injustice. After all, the order came directly from God.

Although Maria again produces witnesses who swear that she was in another place at the time of the theft, she is sentenced to several months in prison.

It is all one big conspiracy against her and her movement, Maria is firmly convinced of that. And she knows a guilty person who started the whole ball rolling: Ernst Venelius. The police officer who never stops asking questions. This young investigator, who is not well-disposed towards her anyway, wants to finish her off. The trial for the perjured false testimony of her supporters in Kokkola is still going on and meanwhile national courts are dealing with the case.

Is it at this time that the cult leader decides that the troublesome Venelius must disappear? Maria starts writing letters - to Eino Vartiovaara, her foster father and most loyal follower, who is completely in bondage to her. In these letters she speaks of revelations that come directly from God. She draws a pistol next to her words. An unmistakable message. Vartiovaara understands.

The former forester hires a hit man. But he betrays him, grabs the money and disappears. In a second attempt, Maria's followers attach a bomb to Venelius' motorboat - but they lack expertise, so the explosive device fails to detonate.

But then January 1924 arrives, and the third attempt hits Venelius hard. Four men from Maria's closest circle of confidants lie in wait on the shore off Kokkola behind some warehouses. When Venelius passes by in his motorboat with his father and sister, they open fire. Four bullets hit Venelius, two his sister; the father remains unharmed. When other boaters who are on the water at that time hear the father's screams, they rush to the aid of the three.

While the first responders do everything they can to save the lives of the wounded, the four masked Åkerblom companions make off down the shore. Venelius and his sister are taken to the hospital by the rushing ambulance. There the doctors fight for their lives. With success. Both recover from the assassination attempt. The four assassins manage to escape. For two days, the police searched intensively for the perpetrators - and caught them less than 48 hours after the crime in a small town in the center of Finland. During interrogation, the shooters claim to have received instructions for the attack directly from Maria Åkerblom.

The investigation into the case has dragged on for years. The close-knit group of followers around Maria and her lies keep delaying a conviction. Her foster father Eino Vartiovaara is not arrested until about three years later as a suspected accomplice in the murder conspiracy against Venelius. By this time, Maria is already in prison as a result of the accusations. She repeatedly tries to escape from captivity. For example, during a prisoner transport by train: she supposedly has to go to the toilet and disappears into the small, narrow room. There, at full speed, she opens the window to jump out of the train into the middle of the icy snowy landscape. Only after several hours is she discovered by an officer in a tree. Freezing through, she had been hiding there.

The media gratefully pick up on such attempts by the "prophetess" to escape. In this way, Maria gains a reputation as a notorious criminal. Her most spectacular escape attempt took place in June 1927.

Maria was imprisoned in Kokkola. She hates the days in prison and longs for freedom. But even in prison she manages to use her skills. As a prisoner, she enjoys a special status because she is always able to convince her wardens to grant her privileges. Among other things, she actually manages to get a wooden bathtub in her cell. The guards think nothing of it.

In June 1927, on an ordinary weekday, one of the guards makes his routine rounds and is horrified to discover that Maria has disappeared. Along with one of her followers, who was housed in the cell next door. The guards discover a large hole under the bathtub that leads to the basement of the prison. This is where the two escaped. In the aftermath, it turns out that a car had then picked up the fugitives outside the prison and taken them to Tampere, a city about 180 km north of Helsinki.

Maria's destination: her movement's villa in Helsinki. From Tampere, she manages to get all the way there in a laundry basket via express delivery. She is slim enough to hide among the laundry. No one notices anything.

It's not a particularly good idea to return to the movement's headquarters. Although she is likely to receive a warm welcome there, after ten days the police show up looking for Maria right there. Maria Åkerblom is arrested again and transferred to prison.

Only one month later, in July 1927, Maria and Eino are finally sentenced by law: Both to 15 years in a labor camp for incitement to murder and perjury. Several other members of the Åkerblom movement are also convicted. Later, their sentences are reduced to 12 years (Vartiovaara) and 8 years

(Maria). Maria serves her sentence in a women's prison located about an hour from Helsinki. Here, too, she tries to escape several times. However, she never succeeds.

The cult leader does everything she can to lead and guide her movement even from prison. She writes numerous letters in which she passes on alleged revelations. In the early years, many still stick by her, the influence of her teachings in the years before had been too strong. The group lives largely isolated on the estate in Helsinki. And everything that has happened can be interpreted in the light of the fact that the last years before the apocalypse have dawned. The hostilities, the perjuries, the attempted murders, the thefts, the arrests, the sentences. The faithful are still firmly convinced that Mary is a prophetess sent by God. What holds them together is the belief that God would soon complete his work. In addition, the followers are strongly influenced by how Maria and Eino bound them to themselves with psychological and physical violence throughout the years before.

But as time goes by, the group breaks apart without the two leading figures. Increasingly, there are believers who turn away. Shortly before Maria is finally dismissed early in 1933, there is a split in the group. A large part turns its back on the movement and joins other churches. In addition, another sleep preacher named Hilda Hottis preaches to the followers and calls Maria a "false prophetess". Many believe her, because even after years they are still waiting in vain for the apocalypse that Mary had announced.

When Mary is finally released from prison, she can no longer maintain her status as a preacher and prophetess, although she tries several times. Few remain faithful to her, and even the close bond between Maria and Eino was never to become what it once was. The Åkerblom movement as a new religious movement with many followers is history.

From then on, Maria concentrated on business activities - quite successfully. Maria still has the ability to convince others. And she plays it out. Soon she is working with a businessman named Lindquist, who is active in the parquet industry. She also manages a farm where she forces some of her few remaining followers to work for her. Under miserable conditions. When Lindquist dies, she takes over his business and continues to run it until it finally goes bankrupt in 1978.

While Maria is successful and secure in the business and financial spheres, she crashes in her private life. She becomes an alcoholic and forces the handful of followers who remain loyal to her for a long time to buy alcohol for her and to always serve her faithfully. Maria Åkerblom lives a dissolute life during this time. She keeps her followers like slaves. They often have to suffer hunger and thirst.

When Maria Åkerblom dies on February 25, 1981, the last remnant of her world collapses for her remaining followers. Maria leaves them nothing, not a cent. Not even the most loyal among them, whom Maria had bound to her and made dependent with decades of psychological violence.

CHAPTER 6

Money problems

Mira Kulla is a light sleeper. "Job-related," she claims herself, and a little pride resonates in her voice every time. Her job brings ups and downs, just like any other job. But other than that, her job can't be described as ordinary at all. For over 40 years, she has been the domestic servant of silk mogul Wilhelm Högsten. She has accompanied a large part of his career as well as the developments of his private life. She has watched his sons and daughters grow up and did not leave his side when he had to return to life partially paralyzed after a tragic accident. Now, Wilhelm is 77 years old and retired. Mira, 60, is not yet thinking about her own retirement. The beautiful, secluded villa and Wilhelm Högsten are her home. She has spent more than half of her life here and doesn't know much outside. As a young girl, she was still afraid of the sounds of the villa at night. It is far outside, isolated in Jollas, a posh suburb of Helsinki. The nearest neighbors live hundreds of meters away, and the estate can only be reached by a single road. Surrounding her are forests, untouched nature that are the natural habitat of a wide variety of animals. She also had to get used to these sounds. Today Mira is no longer afraid. But she has not given up the light sleep. She is always on standby in case her needy master of the house needs her help. So today, April 24, 1992, she is still only lightly dozing in her big, soft bed in the silk sheets. When she hears the noise at about 4:20 a.m., she is immediately wide awake. She instantly understands that these noises are not coming from a trotting deer or the old water pipes. Mira feels her heart beating violently against her chest and fears it might tear her apart. But she doesn't have time to worry about herself now. Quick-witted, she runs up the stairs to the second floor with her flashlight in hand, where her superior's bedroom is located. She calls out his name loudly but receives no response. Then she does something she has never dared to do during her long stay at the mansion - she opens the door to the master's bedroom without knocking. Immediately, heavy air hits Mira, constricting her throat even more than fear already does. Despite the flashlight, she can barely see her hand in front of her eyes, the air is stuffy, it smells like gunpowder. The large balcony door is smashed in. Mira suspects the worst. She quickly dashes forward to the large four-poster bed, in the last hope that she might have been mistaken. But she was right. The sounds that woke her a few minutes ago were actually gunshots. Wilhelm Högsten lies lifeless in his bed.

Her profession has taught her to react with presence of mind even in difficult situations. And even if this isn't a spilled carafe of wine during a business dinner, Mira doesn't lose her head. She rushes to the phone and presses the buttons hard, harder and harder, to call the police and an ambulance. But all she hears is a drawn-out tone. The phone line is no longer working. This can't be a coincidence. The thought that the killer must have snuck past her room with his gun to cut the lines makes her freeze with fear. Mira has to get help. In her long nightgown and slippers, she runs as fast as she can through the night. Only after a few minutes, which seem like hours to Mira, does she reach the nearest neighbor. She screams, knocks vigorously on the massive wooden door, rings the doorbell - until, after what feels like an eternity, a man in silk pajamas opens the door. Shocked by the sight of the old lady standing before him, completely out of breath and in tears, he lets her enter and uses his phone.

Twenty minutes after the shots are fired, police and ambulance arrive at the scene. No trace of the perpetrator can be found. The emergency services quickly analyze the scene: Wilhelm Högsten is dead, shot with three bullets. A fourth bullet missed him and is now lying on the dark wooden floor. The ammunition is 7.63 caliber, a rarity in Finland but common in Russia. The perpetrator left no fingerprints or footprints, and investigators cannot locate any other DNA. The entire estate is full of valuables. Fine furniture, sculptures and original paintings on the walls - but the perpetrator did not steal anything. He did not have robbery in mind. And the smashed balcony door to the bedroom was no accident either. The perpetrator knew exactly where the old man was at night. It was a clear and precisely executed mission: the assassination of Wilhelm Högsten.

Within a few hours, roadblocks are set up in the entire surrounding area. As soon as the sun rises, the investigators start questioning the neighbors. But they know from the start how unlikely it is to find any clues - the properties of the "neighbors" are all hundreds of meters away from the crime scene. They are all the more surprised when they receive a tip from Markus, of all people, one of Högsten's sons. Without hesitation, he accuses his brother, Fred Högsten. He is the prodigal son of the family who, despite having a doctorate in economics, has already lost several thousand Finnish marks. His lifestyle is eccentric, he hardly ever shows up at his parents' house. At birthdays and Christmas parties, his seat was regularly left empty - only when he was financially at a loss did he ever turn up in his father's office. Immediately before his death, Wilhelm Markus had called and reported such an incident. Once again, Fred had come to him with debts of over 1,000,000 marks. He had demanded that Wilhelm sell his villa in order to be able to raise this sum. When his father refused, Fred threatened him and became physically abusive.

That same day, investigators contact Fred, who shows up at the police station promptly. Sitting across from the officers is a nervous man in his early 30s with tousled blond hair, a mustache and horn-rimmed glasses. He speaks quickly, without taking a breath. He admits that his father had lent him money from time to time and that he is currently having financial problems. But that was no reason to murder his own father. He had nothing to do with it. The investigators arrest Fred on urgent suspicion of murder but must release him again after a week due to a lack of evidence.

A few days after Fred's release, the investigators in the Wilhelm Högsten murder case receive a phone call. It is Lana, a daughter of the dead man. She says her brother Fred visited her in her apartment in Helsinki to talk about her father's inheritance. He seemed strange to her, talking only about this one subject, not even asking how she was doing after the tragic incident. When Lana informed him that the inheritance could not be paid out until the murder case was solved, Fred took his leave, saying, "I have to go now, settle a few things."

Immediately, investigators make their way to Fred's apartment with a search warrant. He lets them enter without protest, but keeps affirming, "I already told you everything." The search lasts less than fifteen minutes. On Fred's desk are two sheets of A4 paper with writing on them. They are letters that have not yet been bagged. One is addressed to a friend in Estonia, the other to a man named Slava in Russia. Both letters can be read through quickly and have the same content. Fred asks the men to organize someone who would go to jail for murder for a fee.

Viko and Dima are the names of the men Fred had hired to kill his father in Russia. The contract killing was worth 60,000 marks to him. In preparation, he had made floor plan drawings of the villa and marked exactly where the bedroom was located. He entrusted the documents to a friend of his in Russia to pass on. This friend is one of the addressees of the letters found in Fred's apartment. Slava lives and works near St. Petersburg as a doctor, so the Russian authorities become involved. Never before had Finnish and Russian investigators worked together - like any new thing, this cooperation brings some difficulties. First and foremost, bureaucracy delays progress in the murder case. Before every interview and every business trip, a number of papers have to be filled out and the originals sent by mail across the country's borders. So it takes days for Russian investigators to arrive in Jollas to inspect the crime scene. They are able to confirm that the ammunition used is indeed Russian, but otherwise discover no new leads. On the ground in St. Petersburg, the investigation is also proceeding slowly. There is no trace of the contract killers Viko and Dima. The letter recipient, Slava, remains silent about the incident. He knows Fred, they are friends, but he has never heard of a contract killing or Viko and Dima.

Benti Hervanen is leading the investigation of the Wilhelm Högsten case in Finland. For days he has found it difficult to get up in the morning. He loves his work - actually. But things are just not moving forward in this murder case. Cooperation with Russia is slow, and the great distance and lack of personal contact between the police teams make it difficult to solve the case. Several weeks have already passed since the crime. The more time that passes after a murder, the more difficult it becomes to reconstruct the course of events and catch the perpetrator. That's the theory Hervanen learned during his training. But what happens in practice when the circumstances are so extraordinary? Police cooperation between Russia and Finland has never happened before. Benti Hervanen's displeasure turns into new energy when he hears that the Russian Interior Minister is in Helsinki on a state visit. He pulls out all the stops to meet the politician in person. The politician is open and interested. He promises the Finnish investigator that he will speed up the proceedings.

Only three days later, Hervanen receives a fax from St. Petersburg. The Russian investigative team has questioned Slava again, this time more rigorously, and obtained new, crucial information. According to his testimony, Viko and Dima, the contract killers, do not exist. The truth, he said, was that Fred wanted his father dead. The invented contract killers were meant to cover the trail and distract from the real killer. At this point, the investigation into Wilhelm Högsten's death becomes complicated once again, because according to Slava's stories, another actor comes into play.

When Fred was broke again, he had taken a job with a cab company. There he met a driver named Ilpo Larha. Ilpo Larha is in his early 20s and, despite his negative reputation, is not on the police's books. Apart from a couple of fines for fare evasion, there is nothing against him. However, the young Finn is known for his loud, eccentric and aggressive nature. His great passion is firearms of all kinds. He is a permanent guest at the shooting range in Helsinki, where he spends many hours shooting. According to Slava, Ilpo learned about Fred's murderous plan during a joint visit to Russia with Fred. At that time, Fred was actually looking for men for the job in Slava's home country. But Ilpo beat him to it, saying, "I don't want the money to go to the Russians."

During his interrogation, Ilpo denies the accusations. It is true that he was in Russia with Fred. He also met Slava as Fred's friend. But he, a murderer? No way.

The investigators around Benti Hervanen are not ready to give up so quickly the hot lead they found after months of hard work and back and forth with their Russian colleagues. Benti would stake his life on the fact that Ilpo and Fred are jointly responsible for the murder of Wilhelm Högsten. A spoiled son whose wealth has gone to his head, ultimately driving him to economic ruin. In addition, Ilpo, against whom nothing is on record, but with whom the experienced investigator can't shake the feeling that he would kill with a clear conscience. Moreover, Larha's passion for firearms no longer has much to do with a hobby; he spends every free minute at the shooting range and wanted to know exactly what caliber Högsten was hit with. Hervanen gets an idea: he invites the two of them together for questioning. Fred doesn't seem very loyal to him, and for a reduced sentence he might turn in his accomplice.

And that's exactly how it happens. Benti asks Fred only one question in the small, dark interrogation room: "Is Ilpo Larha your father's murderer - yes or no?" Fred answers, without hesitation, "Yes." Ilpo looks nervously from Hervanen to Fred, but says not a word as he is led away to his cell.

The next day, Ilpo is more cooperative. He tells of a bill collector who had taken 80,000 marks from him. This debt, however, was not his own, but that of a friend named Hannu Ratia. The latter could not pay and sent the bill collector to Ilpo instead. Benti remains silent, lost in his thoughts. If Ilpo's story is true, they are almost certainly dealing with two perpetrators. Ilpo would not pay off a friend's debt and then earn the money back with a murder completely unselfishly.

On July 15, 1992, four armed policemen knock on Hannu Ratia's apartment door. But the full armor turns out to be superfluous: the wanted man opens his door to the task forces a few moments after their arrival and remains calmly standing in a corner while the policemen search the apartment. In addition to Ratia, his girlfriend and another man are also on the scene and behave cooperatively. The investigators quickly find what they are looking for: A revolver lies under the couch. In the bedroom, they find a large sports bag containing more revolvers, smaller pistols and a machine gun, all loaded, with countless large banknotes in between. All three people present are taken into custody.

The second man from Hannu Ratia's apartment is Yarin Neami, a notorious bank robber, but the investigators have to let him go quickly. Neither do the weapons belong to him, nor is there any apparent connection between Neami and Fred Högsten or Ilpo Larha. Ratia quickly admits that he had obtained the firearms for a planned bank robbery. Ilpo's story about his debts is true. The two are friends, he says, and they know each other from the shooting range in Helsinki. But he had nothing to do with the murder of old Wilhelm Högsten.

Meanwhile, in Russia, Slava is communicative when the investigators there inform him about the latest developments in Finland. He tells them that Fred gave Ilpo the job after Ilpo offered himself for it. Ilpo had bragged to Slava and other friends in Russia that he would soon be doing an important job. One that was sure to make the TV news. After his job was done, he told the gruesome details to anyone in St. Petersburg who wanted to know. The housekeeper was right, the phone lines had indeed been cut. The cutter used, Ilpo disposed of at a designated spot in the nearby lake.

In Jollas, the police divers do not have to spend long under the ice-cold water, after a few minutes they find two cable cutters at the described spot. Investigator Benti Hervanen neatly places the devices on the table in the interview room without saying anything about them. After Ilpo enters the room and can't tear his eyes away from the table, Benti is sure. "Why don't you just tell me the whole story?"

And Ilpo Larha does talk, recounting the detailed background and course of events. Benti listens intently for several hours and realizes that the murder occurred more or less as he had put it together: Fred equipped Ilpo with all the important information - floor plans of the villa, exact location of his father's bedroom and the telephone lines. But Ilpo did not think of carrying out the murder alone. He brought Hannu on board - after all, it was about his debts. He was able to convince Fred that the plan would be safer to carry out in pairs. Högsten's son agreed and offered both men half a million Finnish marks each for the job. Ilpo Larha and Hannu Ratia behaved in a remarkably professional manner: they opened various pistol bullets and made their own gunpowder to cover up the caliber of the murder weapon. To get there, they used Hannu's car, whose license plate they had exchanged for that of an identical car an hour earlier, and whose tires they changed the very next day. Hervanen gulps as he realizes that without Ilpo's confession, he might never have been able to solve the knotty case.

The Finnish Supreme Court in Helsinki rules the trial of Fred Högsten, Ilpo Larha and Hannu Ratia in March 1993, handing out the longest prison sentences for a single crime in Finnish criminal history: life for all three perpetrators. As Ilpo is led out of the courtroom in handcuffs by a police officer, he says, "I will not serve my time."

In fact, Ilpo has been in prison for barely a year when he has a pistol smuggled into Helsinki County Jail through acquaintances on February 25, 1994. Together with his new friend, Kullervo Haikas, who is serving 13 years for several drug offenses, he takes a guard hostage. The three of them leave the prison walls behind them - Ilpo doesn't look back. The only way that counts is forward. He threatens the first woman he sees on the road with a gun and steals her car. With the gas pedal to the floor, Ilpo drives on, undeterred, on and on. After several kilometers, he leaves the guard behind at the edge of a forest and drives on towards freedom with Kullervo in the passenger seat.

Ilpo sits on a black leather sofa and smokes a cigarette. His leg bobs up and down restlessly. A week ago, he escaped from prison, and it felt good. He'd never done drugs before, but that's what it had to feel like when people used the phrase "like being high." He felt downright "high," probably the adrenaline. Who would have thought that breaking out of jail would be so easy? That it would be so child's play to smuggle a gun inside the state's locked walls? Sneering, he exhales the cigarette smoke through his nose. The state and the justice system. Without his confession, they would never have found out about him. But even then, when he had told everything to this investigator, he felt it. The tingling in his belly, slowly pushing its way up and then making its way out in excited words. He was proud of what he had done. And in the policeman's eyes he had seen that he was right. Without him, old Högsten would have gone down in history as an unsolved murder case. But now he sits here, in the stuffy, far too cramped den of this drug-addicted woman. She is an acquaintance, or rather a customer, of Kullervo. Together with her and her boyfriend they live here and constantly step on each other's toes. Ilpo feels locked up. He longs for the feeling of absolute freedom, just like last week. Determined, he stubs out his cigarette in the overflowing, smelly ashtray and grabs his gun.

"Bank robbery at SYP Bank in Helsinki, perpetrators on the run." That's the breaking news story on the Finnish news in early March 1994. An employee was shot at, but miraculously the bullet only brushed her hair. Except for a severe shock, she had escaped without any damage. When the police officers interrogate the witnesses, they recognize Ilpo Larha in the descriptions. Since his escape, this is the first and only sign of life they have of him. They now know that Ilpo is probably in the vicinity. In addition, the investigators have recently been in contact with a young woman who is an acquaintance of Ilpo's fellow fugitive, Kullervo. She regularly bought drugs from him. The woman lives in an apartment building in Lahti, about an hour from Helsinki. It's a faint lead, but it's the only one investigators have.

On March 15, 1994, armed police officers in full riot gear make their way to the second floor of the apartment building in Lahti. Ilpo, as a convicted murderer, is considered highly dangerous, and the armed bank robbery has clearly demonstrated his willingness to shoot. Using the apartment's central key, Sula Alda, the head of operations, opens the apartment door. With a shield in front of him, he moves quickly forward towards the living room, where he sees Kullervo Haikas sitting on a black leather sofa. The apartment is tiny, Kullervo was already in Sula's field of vision after opening the door, which is now clouded by cigarette smoke. The air is stuffy and after a few seconds another substance is added: gunpowder. Ilpo Larha peeks out from behind the room's second sofa and immediately opens fire with two revolvers. "Retreat!" orders Sula and the policemen head back to the stairwell. But Ilpo doesn't think of dropping his weapons just because the officers are retreating. There it is again, the rush. He is addicted to the feeling of power that firearms offer him. Laughing loudly and firing, he follows the officers and sees a bullet break off the edge of Sula's shield, hitting him in the torso. Ilpo, even though the man does not go down. The bullet was not fatal. Ilpo feels like a western hero during the wild shootout, like the terror of the big city prairie, superior to all. These officers can't get anything done. They have found him, but he will not go back to jail. He's more likely to blow up the building. He has already made the preparations for this after his bank robbery in Helsinki. It's amazingly easy to build a powerful bomb yourself. Most people would be amazed if he told them that they probably already have all the materials for it at home.

Esko Heinonen is on his way out of work when he gets the news that Ilpo Larha has shot at police officers in Lahti. He is aware that he must not start his journey home now - as a mediator, he is called to the scene of the crime a few minutes later.

When Esko arrives at the residential area in Lahti, the entire area has already been evacuated. Ilpo shoots and shouts from the window of the small apartment on the fourth floor that he would blow up everything if someone entered the building again. Esko takes a deep breath. "The man is obviously crazy," he thinks. It was going to be a long night.

In fact, the mediator is in for several grueling days and nights. Ilpo terrifies the police officers and residents who had to leave their homes for a total of 55 hours. Around 100 police officers are holding the fort, ready for action, and emergency doctors are on standby. Using a SIM phone transported up to the window via a basket, Ilpo demands drinks, food and a getaway car. Esko and his team know that they will lose the convicted murderer again if they provide him with the car. Who knows how far he would go then - none of them wants to bear that responsibility. With them in the apartment still are the young woman who owns the apartment and her boyfriend. And Kullervo. The latter is eagerly talking to the media, who have meanwhile made their way to the scene of the crime despite the cordon. Newspapers, television stations and the radio are so abundant that Esko is surprised that the hustle and bustle hasn't already started stepping on each other's toes. Kullervo reports to the media after a few hours that Ilpo is now also holding him hostage. When he tried to take a gun, Ilpo threatened him with his revolver. Ilpo had gone completely crazy, his mood changing by the minute. All three people present in the apartment fear for their lives.

The next day, March 16, 1994, Ilpo continues to insist on his getaway car, otherwise he would blow everything up. Esko tries his best, but the man on the other end of the line is no longer sane. His biggest concern is the hostages. He bears a great responsibility for their lives as a police mediator. But when he asks Ilpo to let them go so that the two of them can find a solution in peace afterward, Ilpo laughingly replies, "I wouldn't even let the cat get out of this apartment."

On the night of March 17, 1994, emergency personnel sleep in rotation. Mattresses have been brought into the surrounding evacuated buildings so that they can recharge their batteries after more than 45 hours. This is sorely needed. At 5:30 in the morning, Esko's phone rings. Hastily, he picks it up, hoping it's Ilpo. But on the other end of the line, he hears another voice, that of Kullervo. Ilpo has fallen asleep. The policemen must do something, otherwise he would kill them all. Thanks to his experience, Esko can immediately hear from Kullervo's voice that he is not bluffing. The danger is deadly serious.

Esko and the task force are working at full speed. They have to use the time when Ilpo is asleep to free the hostages - a difficult task. The front door is eliminated as a possibility since Ilpo has threatened to use booby traps. A crane upstairs would make too much noise and probably wake the hostage taker. Esko looks up and guesses. The balcony of the fourth-floor apartment is about 4.5 meters above the ground. A jump would not be fatal; at most, one would break a few bones.

The police officers move the mattresses they were sleeping on just a few hours earlier under the balcony. At 6:30 a.m. the owner of the apartment appears on the balcony, looks down and shakes her head vigorously. Over the phone, Kullervo informs Esko that they all would not jump. It is too high, he says. Before the mediator can inform Kullervo that if they don't jump, it will mean their certain death, there is a short, bright scream. The woman lands on the mattresses, gets up crying, and is picked up by a paramedic. Meanwhile, Esko watches as a young man throws a cat down and then jumps himself. At 7 a.m., Kullervo finally overcomes his fear of heights and jumps into his newfound life.

A few minutes later, Ilpo calls Esko. He is beside himself with rage. However, he also admits that the idea of jumping was a clever move. Esko's mind flashes back to how unpredictable Ilpo is. He has to be careful with him. Without the hostages, he seems to completely lose his mind. "7:25 is the deadline. If I don't have a car by then, I'll shoot myself in the head." Esko's attempts to keep 26-year-old Ilpo on the phone fail. He hears a crackle and then the line goes dead.

Immediately, specialists check the front doors for explosives and clear the way after a few minutes. Inside the apartment, they find Ilpo Larha lying lifeless on the floor. Blood is running from his head onto the wooden floor. He shot himself in the head with two pistols at the same time. Next to him is a sports bag with several high explosive homemade bombs.

In 2005, Hannu Ratia is pardoned by Finnish President Tarja Harlonen. He experienced a divine revelation during his time in prison and continues to do religious work in Finnish prisons to this day. In 2006, 14 years after the murder of Wilhelm Högsten, the president also pardoned Fred Högsten, who was responsible for his death. Since then, the millionaire's son has not committed a crime.

CHAPTER 7

I just want to talk

D addy!" the little girl calls out, running to meet him joyfully. Her brown pigtails bob up and down while she holds on to the straps of her pink backpack with her little hands. His heart warms, he smiles. Once again, he realizes how lucky he is with his daughter. He loves his child and thinks she is very special. And indeed, Veera is truly exceptional. She is only six years old. The girl's warm, affectionate nature is already enchanting the whole village. Her friendly, brown eyes light up when she talks to other people. When Marko's daughter smiles, they too smile. Most people just pucker their mouths when she does. But Veera is a true sunshine. Her warmth radiates outward and has enveloped him in indescribable fatherly feelings for six years. Now he is in the car picking her up from kindergarten. Hastily, the father checks one last time: the pistol is loaded and ready in the glove compartment. This afternoon he has to snuff out Veera's light.

As Mari gets off the train, she takes a deep breath. The many cars, shopping malls, bars and skyscrapers have their very own smell. She smells the city. Ivalo is located in Lapland, northern Finland, and its population of just under 3,000 is not comparable to Helsinki or Tampere. Ivalo residents probably wouldn't even call their place of residence a "city." But for 19-year-old Mari, it is. Her home village is a few kilometers away and is characterized by the fact that everyone knows everyone else. The village has a bakery and a butcher. If you want to go to school or to a dentist, you have to go to the next larger village. Mari loves the coziness of her home, but just as much she appreciates escaping it sometimes. She then gets on the train and goes to Ivalo, as she did today. Her friend is already waiting for her at their favorite bar. It is Friday, the weekend is coming and Mari feels free.

The meeting doesn't last long, after an hour Mari's friend says goodbye again. Actually, the two have a lot to tell each other. Mari has just completed her training as a church youth worker and is looking forward to the future. She loves people in all their facets and lives for social contact. The profession of youth worker is made for her. But today her friend only learns superficial facts about all this. Ever since Mari was offered a beer by the attractive stranger, she can no longer concentrate on any conversation. Again and again, her light blue eyes wander from her friend and fix on the strong shoulders of the dark-haired stranger, his broad laugh and height. He must be older than her. Mari feels flattered. As he walks casually and slowly toward her, not a minute after her friend has left the bar, her heart beats faster and faster. She feels her cheeks flush, she nervously twirls one of her dark brown hair strands, and her stomach tightens expectantly. She feels it, the beginning of her very great love.

The unknown man from the bar is called Marko. They get to know each other, friendship turns into love, and the two finally move in together after a few months. Mari leaves her home village and moves in with him in Ivalo, the beloved escape of her youth. Ever since that evening in the bar, Mari has been floating on clouds. She still can't believe that a man like Marko is interested in her. He is in his mid-20s, has a well-paid job and carries her on his hands. Before her move, not an hour went by without news from him. He always wanted to know where she was, what she was doing and who was with her. If she didn't hear her cell phone or couldn't answer his text messages at the moment, he called her directly. He cared about her. It shows even now that they live together. Mari has already introduced him to some of her friends. She was looking forward to it because she loves having people around. In the new apartment, she can now share everything with Marko. They could cook together with friends, have game nights and barbecue in the summer. But Mari soon realizes that a relationship doesn't seem to work that way. Marko finds fault with each of her male friends. A friendship between a man and a woman doesn't work anyway, he says. Secretly, the men would be in love with her or want to sleep with her. He doesn't want to share her and would rather use the time together with her alone. That would be better for them as a couple. When Mari hears this argument, she is initially shocked. She hadn't thought of it that way at all. But Marko is, after all, a man himself and has already gained a few more years of life experience than she has. He sits next to her on the sofa and watches her delete her friends' contact information from her cell phone. Mari is grateful to have a loving partner who cares about her.

After a year of relationship, Marko asks Mari the all-important question. Mari is overjoyed, she knows only one answer: yes, she wants to become Marko's wife. Now and forever.

Most days in their marriage are the same, a routine creeps in. The newly married couple leaves the house for work. Afterwards, Mari comes straight home and prepares something for her husband to eat. They spend their evenings together on the sofa. When a friend tells her that they don't see each other anymore, Mari is confused. After all, her friend has a husband, so she should know better. Close friendships have no place in a serious relationship. When she tells Marko about it, he asks her to delete her friend's cell phone number from her phone. And some other female contacts, too, whom he considers a bad influence. When Marko takes her in his arms afterwards, for the first time the familiar feeling of safety does not settle inside Mari. She is too warm in his arms; she can't breathe properly.

Later in the week, Mari is in the kitchen preparing a lemon cake. Lost in thought, she cracks an egg and watches it drop onto the butter and sugar mixture. She yawns and lets her head circle slowly back and forth. She is tired, having not been able to sleep properly for days. First it's thoughts of Marko and their marriage that keep her awake, and then he himself when he snores too loudly. There have been frequent arguments in the last few days. Mari feels uncomfortable. Her young life is going along well-worn paths, and it is quiet. The emptiness inside her crushes her. Her cell phone no longer rings, and when it does, it's Marko, a colleague who wants to trade shifts with her, or someone in her family. No one sends her photos from the weekend trip anymore, no one remembers her birthday. She no longer knows anything about the people who used to be her friends. After dinner, it has become routine for Marko to search her cell phone. He is convinced that she is hiding something from him or even having an affair with another man. She wonders what he does with her phone during the 20 to 30 minutes, since she doesn't receive any more messages or calls anyway.

When Mari realizes that she forgot the lemons at the supermarket, her stomach tightens painfully. Surely Marko would see a connection to some alleged secrecy in this mistake as well. She doesn't want to tell him, because then he would surely want to come with her. Today she has no more strength to go through this ordeal. Because whenever Marko goes shopping with her, she has to be extra vigilant. If she sees a colleague or neighbor, she changes aisles as quickly as possible under a pretext. She avoids any contact, even if it is only a greeting. Because she can't stand Marko's questions afterwards: Who is he? How do you know him? Why does he know you? Why does he greet you? Did you smile at him? Mari decides that there will be no lemon cake for dessert tonight. Fortunately, she hasn't announced it to Marko yet, she thinks with relief.

The young couple has wanted a baby since the beginning of their relationship. After the wedding, Mari had stopped taking birth control pills, but she didn't get pregnant for a year. Today, on a cool autumn day in 2011, she has been sitting motionless on the toilet for half an hour. In her hand, she holds a plastic strip that displays two blue lines. The pregnancy test is positive, they are having a baby.

After the initial speechlessness, Mari regains her composure. The last time was not always easy, but Marko is still the man she fell head over heels in love with back then and whom she eventually married. The man who provides for her, and in the future, for her little family. Maybe now is just the right time to have a child. Surely the news would soothe Marko and set their marriage on the right track.

When Marko comes home that day, he greets her with a question. In the driveway, he has seen fresh tire tracks in the snow, even though it is already snowing heavily today for a day in the fall. I wonder if she left the house again after work. And if so, why? Mari denies it, but immediately regrets it when

Marko continues to probe who else the tire tracks are from. Whether someone visited her? Mari has no answer for that, she doesn't know whose car hit her driveway. She swallows hard and decides to lie. She said she heard a van and looked out the window. She saw the van make a U-turn in her driveway. Before any more doubts can hail, Mari spontaneously grabs her husband's hands and smiles at him. "We're having a baby. I'm pregnant," she says. The hope that is in her voice comes to an abrupt end when Marko runs into the kitchen. He flips back through the calendar and calculates whether he can be the child's father.

In June 2012, Veera is born. Since the day of her birth, Mari sincerely loves her child. She is her everything. Marko, too, is completely infatuated with the little one, Veera is curious and creative. She loves to paint, dance ballet and play with other children. Mari recognizes herself in her and often thinks back to her old friends. She wonders what happened to them. But these thoughts never last long, because they belong to the past. When she looks into Veera's bright eyes, she sees her present and future in them.

When Veera is three years old, the small family moves to a town 13 kilometers east of Ivalo. Marko has bought a new house for the family. Mari notices how much he loves Veera. He plays touchingly with her and gives her small gifts. However, neither Veera nor the move change anything in their marriage. Mari feels more and more worthless. She can't do anything right in Marko's eyes. Her thoughts circle day and night around her behavior and how Marko might react to it. She rethinks each of her actions several times, afraid that her husband might bombard her again with questions and accusations. At one point, she considers that she might catch a virus at the supermarket and infect Marko if she touches the food on the shelves. It is a frightening thought for her. So, from that point on, Mari spends several hours a day washing her hands with lots of soap and hot water. She scrubs until her hands have hematomas.

Again and again, the thought of divorce crosses Mari's mind, and she brings it up with Marko. But he refuses. Marko wants to keep the family together. Mari finally agrees with him. But inwardly she is sure that two separate, peaceful homes would be better for Veera than the one they share, which is under stress, duress and aggression.

In the summer of 2017, Veera has just turned five, Mari and Marko argue again over something small. At that moment, Mari feels a deep conviction that their marriage has finally failed. This is not the life and not the relationship model between husband and wife that she wants to convey to her daughter. In a calm voice, she announces to Marko that she is moving out with Veera and that she wants a divorce.

Marko stays behind while Mari packs her bags with Veera and moves to Ivalo. They share custody - one week the girl lives with her mother and the following week with her father. Both parents agree to this arrangement. Mari thinks that even though their marriage ended unhappily, that Veera needs her father and Marko needs his daughter.

The separation becomes increasingly good for Mari. She feels liberated. Back in Ivalo, she can breathe. She smells it again, the life she perceived back then as a 19-year-old girl already in the city. Her family reacts with shock to the news of the separation. No one noticed anything. To the outside world, the three of them were always the perfect family. Marko, the loving and caring husband and family man, Mari as a warm, young mother and Veera, the charming, fun-loving girl. But soon Mari's family experiences firsthand what Mari had to suffer in her relationship with Marko.

Marko does not accept Mari's wish for a divorce. He writes her text messages incessantly, sometimes 100 a day. He starts in the morning after getting up at six o'clock and doesn't stop until late at night. Most of the time the messages are controlling in nature, he then wants to know what she is doing and if she has met a new man. Just like when they first moved in together, Mari thinks. However, he often insults her and threatens her that no one can have her if not him. On October 24, 2018, Mari contacts the police and asks for a restraining order against Marko. Since there is no direct violence from him, the police cannot issue an immediate no-contact order. The case will be reviewed for the time being, and Mari will be contacted again.

On Monday, October 29, 2018, Marko's cell phone rings at 9:25 am. He always keeps his cell phone close by to respond quickly when Mari calls. So far, that has not been the case. The only contact she allows is the very necessary arrangements regarding their daughter. Today, too, it is not Mari's number on the display, but one that is unknown to him. He answers with his name and then listens for three minutes as if in shock. It is a juror from the Lapland District Court. Mari has obtained a restraining order against him. From now on, he is not allowed to contact her or go near her unless he picks up his daughter at her house. "No," Marko finally presses out, briskly interrupting the employee, "I don't accept that."

Shortly after; Mari is sitting in the office when her cell phone lights up wildly and vibrates. Embarrassed, she switches it to silent so as not to disturb her colleagues. It's Marko. He heard about the restraining order and is now asking her to withdraw it. She emails the police about the news and ignores her cell phone.

After closing time, she rushes to the kindergarten. Another look at her cell phone; she sees that the last message from Marko arrived at 10:37. A missed call and a text message, "I just want to talk to you!" Mari quickly banishes thoughts of her ex-husband from her mind. After a week with her father, Veera returns to her home today. She is happy to embrace her daughter and spend time with her. This afternoon they would like to bake a cake together, and tomorrow she would drive the girl to her beloved ballet class and watch her pirouette playfully in her pink tutu. With a satisfied smile, Mari drives off in the direction of the kindergarten.

Veera is no longer here. The words of the friendly kindergarten teacher unsettle Mari, and even more so what she says afterwards: "Marko picked Veera up at 1 p.m. today." A punch in the face, a kick in the pit of the stomach would be nothing compared to the feeling that now chokes Mari's throat. Instinctively, she knows something is not right here. Veera has afternoon activities on Mondays at kindergarten. In craft class, she is currently working on postcards with autumn themes. Last week they went for a walk together and collected colorful leaves for this purpose and pressed them into Mari's thick novels. The educator, of course, entrusted Marko with his daughter when he said he had another appointment with the girl this afternoon.

Mari drives around the city for twenty minutes. It is the longest twenty minutes of her life, during which there is no trace of Marko or her daughter. At 3:50 p.m., she calls the police. Distraught and worried, the young mother explains the situation to the officers. "Please," she sobs, "bring my daughter back to me."

Mari doesn't wake up again until around noon the next day, when her cousin gently strokes her back. The tears in her eyes remind Mari right back to last night. After her call to the police, she has returned home. She paced restlessly, called Marko several times, but his cell phone was disconnected. When her doorbell rang in the evening and she saw two people standing in her doorway, she immediately knew what was coming. There were two people, but only one of them was a police officer. The woman standing next to the officer was a social worker. Within seconds, Mari realized what that meant. "We found two bodies," she could still hear as if through a tunnel, then she lost consciousness. Now she is lying in her bed, her cousin next to her crying. The police are back, she says, can Mari talk to them? Yes. Mari wants to know what happened; she needs to know. She slowly walks into her living room. She realizes that once she sits across from them on the sofa, there is no turning back. Then reality hits her without warning. As if in a trance, she perceives the policeman and the social worker from yesterday. They have found Veera and Marko dead in his house. In their former family residence. After receiving Mari's call, the police officers directly checked Marko's address and found his car in the driveway. The rear door was open, and a small, pink backpack was visibly sticking out. When officers entered the house at 4:45 p.m., they found two bodies with gunshot wounds to the head directly in the entryway. The door to the boiler room, which led directly off the hallway, was also open. So they quickly discovered the message Marko had left there in big letters with paint on the wall: "Wouldn't it have been worth talking after all?" The investigation does not take long. Quickly the course of events is clear. Marko killed Veera right after entering the house with a shot in the back of the head and then shot himself. He left the message on the wall before picking up his daughter from kindergarten and burned his cell phone in the fireplace. That's why Mari couldn't reach him. There are no other signs of violence. Veera probably did not suspect anything about her father's intention when he picked her up from kindergarten earlier. Marko behaved normally and inconspicuously before the crime. Forensic psychologists later find that after the separation, the father could not develop his own identity and could not accept having to build his own independent life without his wife. He blamed Mari alone for the breakup of the family.

In the months that follow, Mari is never alone. Her sisters and cousins are always with her. They go shopping, make sure Mari eats, showers, and call her in sick at work. The people of Ivalo are shocked by the tragic case of the father who deceitfully and selfishly kills his daughter, who trusted him and was completely at his mercy. To finance the funeral and express their sympathy, the village community is collecting donations.

In November 2018, the funeral service for little Veera takes place in Ivalo. The whole community is present as the small white coffin, carved by Mari's father and her sisters, is lowered into the ground. For Mari, today is the hardest day of her life and the beginning of months of grief and depression. Marko's funeral will be held among immediate family and anonymously.

In the spring of 2019, Mari makes a decision. She wants to live. Because that is what Veera would have wanted for her mother. Her daughter loved life and enjoyed it with every breath. She expressed her joy of life with every pirouette, every painted picture. Marko, on the other hand, wanted to destroy her with his deed. His wish was that she would never again be happy in her life. She does not want to grant him this triumph. She travels, tries out new hobbies and writes an online blog to cope with her grief. Today, she lives in southern Finland with a new man by her side. From time to time, she still blames herself terribly. But therapy has helped her to be milder with herself. She has learned that the only way she could have prevented the drama was an impossible one: she should never have fallen in love with Marko.

CHAPTER 8

Breathless

Absolute darkness surrounds the girl. Her eyes take minutes to get used to the black inside the closet. She feels like she's in a bad dream. Not even an hour ago, 12-year-old Sarah was playing with her best friend Anna. It's July, the sun's rays warmed them pleasantly as they frolicked through nature. They were watching birds and buying strawberry ice cream with their pocket money. But then suddenly there was this man who just ruined their beautiful summer day. Sarah pinches her own wrist, eagerly hoping to wake up and laugh with Anna again without a care in the world. But she is not asleep, this is not a dream. Reality now consists of dust, the musty smell, the cracked wood of the closet and terrible loneliness. For she must crouch alone in the dark, her friend Anna the man has kept outside in his living room. At first, Sarah still heard her loud cries, her frightened voice, and that she was crying. But for a few seconds there has been silence. The little girl suspects: this is just the calm before the storm.

His anger grows more violent by the second, he feels a burning in his stomach and his hands clench into fists. He would have preferred to go through with it himself, alone, as always. Not much longer and all three of them would be caught. And then it would probably mean juvenile detention for him once and for all. This time he would probably not get away with a warning after his numerous thefts, drug histories and violent offenses. Up to now, the most he had been ordered to do was community service, and then he would run around town with a garbage bag and pick up the dirt of others. His life hadn't always been like this. Until a few years ago, he was a model student, friendly and popular. But then his parents divorced, and his mother started bringing home different men all the time. Money was always tight. He quickly aborts the thought, focusing on reality, on the here and now. "Faster, damn it!" 15-year-old Jukka Torsten Lindholm alerts his two classmates that they don't have much time left. His hometown of Oulu in the north of the country is Finland's fifth largest city, and there's always something going on here. Some say a big city offers anonymity. Jukka knows it doesn't. A few weeks ago, he discovered a new source of income - besides taking grandma's checkbook with him - slot machines. They can be found in the late 1970s in every supermarket, in every pub, at some gas stations and in the entrance halls of department stores. Once you get the hang of it, they are child's play to open. He has already earned several hundred Finnish marks doing this, but telling these two idiots from his classmates about it was not a good idea. The two of them take far too long and don't seem to have the right tools with them. They can't work on the machine undetected for long. At first it works well, in the hustle and bustle of the big city a boy handling a slot machine is quickly lost. But three at once and for more than half an hour by now, that's definitely too conspicuous. Wordlessly, Jukka turns on his heel and leaves the other two boys behind. Alone and on his own, he is doing best.

In November 1981, the Finnish winter has long since begun. The days are short, if the sun shows itself at all. It doesn't rise most mornings, so people live in a diffuse black-gray and only know when it's day and when it's night thanks to their watches. Snow falls and many of his acquaintances are annoyed by icy windshields or uncleared train tracks. But Jukka feels comfortable in the cold. Now he can wear his long black coat. In addition, the darkness offers him protection. He can hide and avoid other people noticing him directly. So, he sneaks through the streets of Oulu on weekend evenings and watches people. Most of the time he is warmed by the alcohol from his flask, which he carries with him everywhere in the inside pocket of his coat. Today is Friday and he had already watched the girl through a window, dancing and laughing at this party. She must be his age, 16, not much younger or older. Her shoulder-length black hair swayed in time with her movements, as did her beautiful silk scarf, all the while she smiled. Now, when he overpowers her in the stairwell of the apartment building she had reached within a few minutes' walk after the party, she is no longer smiling. Her eyes widen in fear and she wants to scream, but Jukka holds his cold, big hand in front of her mouth. He pushes her into the elevator and presses the button for the basement floor. The girl is shaking all over, he can't trust her. "One word and you're dead," he therefore threatens her to get her to be quiet. Once in the basement, he pulls the turquoise silk scarf tightly around her neck. After just a few seconds, he feels his pants tighten and get tighter. His friends exchange magazines with each other, featuring tons of naked women. But Jukka doesn't understand what they find in the photos. A few times he tried it too, in his room, at night. He sat naked on his bed, the magazine open in front of him. He touched himself, but nothing moved. Today it is different. He is aroused by strangling the girl. So much so that he is now ready to take a step further. As he keeps banging her head on the hard concrete floor, he repeats in a whisper, "I'm going to rape you now." Jukka unbuckles his belt with both hands and realizes his mistake post-haste. The girl seizes the moment and flees. She is petite and agile; Jukka has no chance to catch her yet. When the girl returns to the scene half an hour later with her friends, there is no trace of her attacker. The next day, the girl describes him at the police station. The officers show her matching photos from the files, in which Jukka is also listed because of his criminal past. She can identify him clearly.

Confronted with the police officers, who went on their way immediately after the girl's report, Jukka admits his crime without resistance. But he does not name a motive. A few months later, in early 1982, he is sentenced to six months' probation, plus he has to pay his victim compensation for pain and suffering.

At the end of his parole, Jukka feels liberated. At last he is no longer under constant surveillance, no longer has to go to weekly appointments at police headquarters. And the meticulous reporting of his every move has also come to an end. He breathes in the fresh air as he stands under cover of darkness in front of an electronics store in town. A rush floods through him as he smashes the glass front with a rock and fills his pockets with computers and phones.

Jukka's freedom was not to last long. He is quickly arrested for burglary, property damage and theft. This time he doesn't get off with a suspended sentence but is sentenced to a year in juvenile detention. In his cell, he counts down every single day. The seconds pass painfully slowly and he finds no contact with the other inmates. Juvenile detention is truly hell for him.

When Jukka is released, he is 20 years old. This means he can now legally consume alcohol and go to bars. And that's exactly what he does. Jukka continues the lifestyle he started when he was 13, drinking, taking drugs and living at the expense of his mother, Laina. He gets along well with Laina, she loves her son. She likes to share her small salary, which she earns as a barmaid, with her boy. Eventually he would get on the right track, he just needs a little more time. While he was in juvenile detention, she met a new man, still newly in love. Shortly after her son's release, she wants to introduce the two men in her life to each other and organizes an evening in a bar. A cozy atmosphere, a beer - the best conditions for a successful meeting. But as so often in life, everything turns out quite differently than planned. Laina and her boyfriend get into a fight over something trivial. Jukka interferes and gets physical with Laina's partner. The evening ends quickly and lonely. Laina and her son return home alone.

The next day, the phone rings in Laina's apartment, but no one picks it up. There is absolute silence, interrupted only by the unanswered ringing. On the other end of the line is a puzzled man whose skepticism slowly turns to concern. It is Jukka's biological father. His son was supposed to come by his house today, but he doesn't show up, even though he didn't cancel. Hours ago, Jukka should have been there and now no one is answering the phone at the apartment. All this is uncharacteristic for his son. Restless, he contacts his ex-wife's brother, who picks up the spare key to Laina's apartment from her mother. When the two men enter the empty apartment, at first it seems that no one is home. No one responds to their calls. Laina should be home during the day, she works night shifts at the bar. Maybe she is resting? The men knock on the bedroom door but again get no answer. When they open the door, Laina is lying on her bed, seemingly asleep. But no human being can be blessed with such a deep sleep that they are not awakened by loud shouts, nor by vigorous shaking. Laina's brother and her ex-husband call the police and an emergency doctor, who confirms what they already suspected: Laina is dead. But how can that be? There is no blood, she has no bruises or other wounds anywhere on her body. According to the doctors' initial assessment, the woman died naturally, falling asleep forever. As comforting as this suspicion may be, the autopsy quickly disproves it. Laina was suffocated.

Both Laina's partner and her son are summoned to police headquarters for questioning. The officers let the completely distraught partner go after a few minutes; he has an alibi and is obviously struggling with the fact that the last encounter with Laina ended in an argument. Jukka, on the other hand, gets tangled up in different stories, jumping from one version to the next. But there is no evidence against him either. The police let the young man go and the case lies unsolved for a year.

July 26, 1986, is one of the rare days in Finland when the sun is shining. It is summer and many Finns are enjoying the warming rays on their skin to the fullest. Some of them put their entire annual vacation into this season. Sarah and Anna don't have to worry about that yet. For the two 12-year-old girls, life is carefree. For them, summer vacation gives them freedom and countless opportunities. The friends spend almost every day together outside in nature. They love to romp, watch birds and eat ice cream. So today, too, they sit on their favorite bench in town, both girls gleefully licking a strawberry ice cream. They talk about school, cute boys, and their often-annoying siblings. How nice that they have each other. Suddenly, the sun disappears from the two fun-loving children's faces. A tall man in long black clothes stands directly in front of them, casting a shadow over their small faces. Sarah and Anna are surprised that the man is not far too warm in his long pants. In each hand he carries a beer crate. He asks the girls if they can help him carry it up to his apartment. He lives not far away, he says, and he would reward their help with a little change. The two girls don't have to think long. With the money they could afford to go swimming tomorrow, how tempting! Without a second thought, they follow the man, not suspecting that he will put an abrupt end to their carefree summer.

As soon as they arrive at the apartment, Jukka closes the door. He invites the girls into the bedroom, where he keeps his small change. They are 12 years old and yet still so naive - Jukka exhales his breath derisively at this thought. At that age, he himself had his first beer, yet the two of them go along with a strange man like toddlers. But enough with the constant thinking. Arriving in the bedroom, he grabs one of them, Sarah, tightly by her small shoulders. How fragile they still are at that age. Immediately the girls begin to scream loudly in fright. "Hush, or you won't get out of here alive!" he threatens them. The harsh words hit home. Sarah lets herself be locked in the closet without resistance. The other one looks at Jukka from below out of brown puppy eyes. A tear runs down one of her full cheeks. "Please..." she starts, but Jukka doesn't listen to her at all. He quickly unbuckles his belt, pulls it out of its buckles, and places it around the girl's small, delicate neck. He manages to wrap it around several times. Anna coughs and gasps, and Jukka excitedly undoes his pants button. Only when the girl falls to the floor does he open the closet and invite the other to lie down next to her motionless friend. Jukka lies down between the children and rubs himself against their small bodies. "Have you ever had sex before? I'm going to have sex with you now," he moans and Sarah suffers agony. Her friend Anna is turning blue in the face and won't open her eyes. An hour ago, they were eating ice cream together and laughing. While still in the dark, smelly closet, she pinched her wrist several times to wake up from this nightmare. But she doesn't stay idle as she understands that she has to act. She jumps up and runs out of the room, down the hall and opens the apartment door, which the man fortunately did not lock. In the stairwell she screams for help and quickly neighbors become aware of the completely distraught girl. When the horrified rescue workers arrive, they find the body of 12-year-old Anna in Jukka's open apartment. There is no trace of the perpetrator.

A few hours later, the emergency services find Jukka in the forest. He tried to escape but did not get far. The sight of him is a source of concern for the police officers. Despite the summer heat, he is wearing a long-sleeved, black top, and his equally long, dark pants are open. His dark blond, long hair is standing out frayed in all directions. He looks at them from dull, light blue eyes, his face completely expressionless, his narrow lower lip pursed constantly. The officers quietly think they are dealing with a maniac, handcuff him and push him into the back seat of their car. During the drive towards the police station, Jukka moves his upper body back and forth and starts talking to himself. He talks about his mother. "Mom would save me, mom would defend me!"

During his interrogation, Jukka confesses that he wanted to have sex with the two girls. However, he says, it was not his intention to kill them. He also starts talking about his mother completely out of nowhere. He had also strangled her, "that whore". He was so angry at her because she couldn't free him from the juvenile detention center. For him it was absolute hell. But she had preferred to build a life with her new partner. Even his stepsister had to move out because the apartment became too small. When he saw Laina lying on her bed that night after the argument, he put on her blue gloves and strangled her with her own red scarf. He didn't report the incident earlier, he says, because it wasn't murder after all - in his mind, Mom still lives on. An hour later, Jukka withdraws his confession, but the court is convinced. In March 1987, the now 22-year-old is sentenced to eight years and six months in prison for the two murders, as well as for rape and deprivation of liberty.

Jukka has served about five years of his sentence when he is released on parole. His grandmother Maria takes in her grandson. For a year, the old lady is sure that Jukka is finally getting on the right track. For a year the police do not pick him up, there are no drug excesses, thefts or even worse. When Jukka's grandmother returns home on a pleasant day in June 1993 after visiting her sister, she is completely lost in these thoughts. At the meeting, she had told her sister how grateful she was for her grandson's positive development. He has not had an easy life and has made many serious mistakes, but things are finally looking up. Maria closes the front door behind her and turns directly to the right, toward a small guest bathroom. She has always washed her hands there when she comes home from outside. For her, this is one of those actions that is so automatic that one doesn't even remember the details afterwards. For example, she only notices the corpse above her toilet when she has already turned on the tap at the sink. At the sight of the completely black-clad figure, of which only the dark-haired back of the head is visible, since the face is hanging in the toilet, a sharp scream escapes Maria. She rushes out of the room and calls the police. The faucet runs until the arriving investigators shut it off. Then there is silence.

The body is a young woman named Eya. Red strangulation marks are clearly visible around her neck, and her face is blue. The investigators immediately know who to question. At first Jukka denies the crime, but after a few minutes he confesses that he only wanted to sleep with Eya. He had revealed his strangulation fetish to her and suggested that they could try it together. Eya didn't say no, he said. That's when he took the towel from the guest bathroom and squeezed it shut. He only let go when Eya fell motionless to the floor. It took him a few seconds to understand what had happened and he panicked. When the doorbell rang, he moved the body to the toilet and reflexively fled to his mother's grave, where he had spent many hours. It had been an accident.

A psychiatric report proves that Jukka is fully responsible for his deed, despite his extreme sexual perversion. Thus, on December 13, 1993, he is sentenced to 10.5 years in prison for the murder of his girlfriend Eya.

Jukka serves two-thirds of his sentence without any special incidents. In 2000, now 35 years old, he begins to wear women's clothes and makeup. The prison warden issues a ban. Future orders for feminine clothing and makeup are stopped. A complaint by Jukka is rejected by the management, for his own protection. Other inmates might feel harassed and provoked. Jukka eventually accepts the ban and quickly reverts to his old style of dress. Instead, he now reinvents himself religiously and with a wife by his side - he becomes a Catholic and marries one of his fellow inmates, Hannele Pentholm, who is serving a life sentence for murdering her husband. In addition to his wife's last name, which Jukka adopts, he also has his first name changed to "Michael Maria." Perhaps all this is meant to represent a new beginning for him. The two convicted murderers remain a couple for several years until

Jukka is released from prison in late 2008. After the divorce, he drops his now ex-wife's last name and changes it once again - from now on he goes through his new life as "Michael Maria Penttilä".

Initially, the time as a free man passes quietly and without criminal conspicuousness. In August 2009 Michael Penttilä's mood changes. He orders a masseuse to visit him at home. Before she can even set up her couch, two leather-gloved, large hands wrap around her neck from behind. Michael forces the terrified woman into his bedroom and pushes her onto his bed, his hands barely leaving her neck. The woman, fearing for her life, knows that Michael is far superior to her physically. Quick-witted, she tries to talk to him. At first, her attacker does not listen to her; he is obsessed with his stranglehold. But after a few long minutes, he actually lets go of her. She strokes his arm motherly and suggests that they have a coffee together and discuss everything. As if in a trance, Michael actually goes to the kitchen, makes two cups of coffee, and talks with the woman whose life he just had in his hands. After an hour, the masseuse says goodbye and leaves his apartment unharmed - at least physically. As a farewell, Michael gives her a kiss on the forehead.

Incidents like this accumulate in the immediate next period. Just one month later, in September 2009, Michael, now 44, hires a cleaning woman and strangles her from behind. She manages to firmly bite his hand and is able to escape. Just three weeks later, Michael attacks another cleaning woman in the same way; she also manages to escape. In his statement to the police, he later affirms that he was terribly lonely and hungry for love. He "just wanted to have some BDSM fun" with the women and not kill them. In June 2010, Michael is sentenced to another six years in prison and must pay the women a total of 7,000 USD in damages for pain and suffering. In a psychiatric report prepared as part of the current trial, Michael is classified as particularly dangerous to society. It strongly advises against converting his imprisonment into a suspended sentence.

Despite the clear warning, Michael enjoys some freedoms in custody. For example, he has regular time off. In October 2015, he does not return from a trip to the mall - he has escaped.

Just one day later, the police are able to apprehend him and take him back to his cell. At Christmas 2016, around four years before the regular end of his prison sentence, Michael is released on parole. Again, against the recommendations of the psychiatric report.

Again, it becomes quiet around Michael at first. He spends his time on dating sites on the Internet and writes to various women. One of them particularly took a fancy to him. Her name is Susi, and she is in her mid-twenties. When he looks at her photos, he is captivated by her long, black hair and her fair-skinned, slender neck. He longs to wrap his hands around it and squeeze. With a scarf or a shawl, he would enjoy it, too.

Michael tries to masturbate to these thoughts, but does not succeed.

One afternoon, Michael looks out the window and sees a girl from the neighborhood. A beauty with long black hair and a slim, trained figure. His happiness is at his feet, she lives in the house just across the street from him. Emi is his neighbor.

In April 2017, 17-year-old Emi looks in the mailbox as she does every afternoon when she returns from school and finds a strange letter. In a spidery, almost childish handwriting, "Susi" is written on an envelope. She doesn't know any "Susi." It is Friday and her parents have gone out. She's bored and curious, so Emi opens the letter, even though she knows you shouldn't open other people's mail. At this point, the teenager has no idea that this very rule-breaking could have saved her life. Shocked, she reads the creepy content: "Hi Susi, if you want to meet and get to know me, let me know. I'm on several dating sites, but I don't like to chat. Most of the time it leads nowhere, and I'm looking for a steady girlfriend, not just a one night stand. I have seen you a few times now. I think you are very pretty, and you have a great body. I'll write down my phone number here in case you want to contact me. You can also call from the window if you want to meet me. I like foreign women. All the best, arrivederci from Michael."

Disgusted, Emi drops the piece of paper. Foreign women? Dating sites? The words make no sense at all. She saves the phone number in her phone, but this Michael guy doesn't seem to use WhatsApp yet. Strange. She finally finds what she is looking for on Instagram and finds a profile called "Leather Glove" linked to the number. Looking at the photos sends a cold shiver down her spine. The thin, frayed hair, the high forehead, and the vacant, maniacal stare. It's him, clearly. The serial strangler has written her a letter. Emi locks all the doors, lowers the blinds, and hides in her room with a kitchen knife. Immediately, she recalls an incident a few months ago. In January, on an evening when her parents had gone out like they did today, she had heard a scratching at the door, as if someone was trying to get in. When Emi looked through the peephole, she saw a man. A scream escaped her, and the man ran away. Maybe that had been the serial strangler, too. Frantically, she looked at her cell phone. She has already called her father a few minutes ago and is now waiting for him to call her back. Tears run down her cheeks. She doesn't want to die. She still has so much to accomplish; her life has only just begun. And now a serial killer has her in his sights. The ringing of her phone makes Emi flinch and brings her back to the present in one fell swoop. She describes to her father what happened, completely out of breath. Her parents immediately make their way back.

The police arrive almost simultaneously with Emi's parents. After the young girl's statement, they cross the street and ring Michael's doorbell. The latter claims that he mistook Emi for Susi from his dating site. But the woman in the photos bears no resemblance to Michael's 17-year-old neighbor. Emi and her parents file a complaint. The court decides that 52-year-old Michael does not have to be remanded in custody until the trial begins. No one had been harmed, it was now a case of testimony against testimony. Michael affirms that he wants to mend his ways and lead a new life. In July 2017, he is acquitted.

While Emi and her parents appeal the acquittal, Michael lives in freedom and awaits the new trial. On April 13, 2018, he buys a prepaid cell phone and calls Linda, a 52-year-old prostitute. He wants to arrange a meeting, preferably for tonight. Linda agrees and invites him to her home. In addition to his long, black clothes, he is wearing sunglasses when he arrives at Linda's. He takes them off only after closing the door behind him. Immediately, the woman recognizes him and panics. "You're the serial strangler! You freak!" In Michael's head, everything stopped. He fixes Linda with his blank stare as he takes off his belt. Then he puts it around the woman's neck and pulls tight. He doesn't let go until Linda is dead. He then lays the body on her bed and stays in the apartment for two days to clean up his tracks. When the body is found three weeks later, on May 4, 2018, investigators can find no DNA or fingerprints at the scene. On Michael's belt, however, they find the victim's DNA.

The autopsy reveals that Linda had a six-to-eight minute, bitter struggle to survive. Her death did not set in briefly and painlessly but was delayed by Michael. When she was on the verge of unconsciousness, he would loosen the pressure on her neck, only to strangle her tighter shortly after.

A few days later, the trial involving 17-year-old Emi resumes. This time, the prosecution obtains a prison sentence of two years and six months, plus 4,000 USD in compensation for Emi's pain and suffering.

In July 2018, Michael is found guilty of Linda's murder and sentenced to life in prison. In addition, he must pay the victim's mother 3,000 USD for the funeral of her daughter and 10,000 USD in damages for pain and suffering.

In 2019, Michael himself requests another psychiatric report. Just like their predecessors, this one also confirms him a pronounced form of sexual perversity. Sexual preferences in the direction of bondage and strangulation are widespread and nothing special given mutual consent. Michael's case represents an extreme form in which he is only capable of sexual intercourse at all through violent and forced strangulation. Whether this diagnosis reduces his culpability and thus his life sentence has not yet been determined. The appeal process is ongoing.

The case of Michael Maria Penttilä still shocks the whole of Finland today. Between the years 1985 and 2018, four people died at the hands of the "serial strangler." The number of women who experienced mortal fear over decades due to his attacks and abuse is incalculable. The case is unique in its cruelty and therefore known beyond the country's borders. Even the FBI has analyzed Michael - and declared him the only known Finnish serial killer to date.

CHAPTER 9

24 Minutes

(By Lisa Bielec / Mordgeflüster the Podcast)

I t is a rather cold, gray and cloudy morning on this Wednesday, November 7, 2007 in the small town of Jokela. Jokela is a small part of the Finnish municipality of Tuusula and is located about an hour's drive north of Helsinki. There are about 6000 inhabitants living here. Many of them use the well-known wooden train station, built back in 1875, to commute from their home village to the surrounding big cities. The rent and real estate prices in the small town are quite affordable, but in return, one also forgoes many amenities that one can use to a sufficient extent in large cities. But that doesn't bother the residents of Jokela. Although there is not much going on here, those who like to live close to nature and seek their peace and quiet are in exactly the right place. It is exactly this quietness and coziness that the inhabitants of the small town appreciate. It's a great way to escape the stress of everyday life. If the weather allows it, people also like to stop at their neighbors to have a nice chat or get an ice cream in the small-town center to comfortably eat it on the way home.

Jokela is a very normal Finnish town, if it wasn't for that one black day that all the inhabitants can remember only too well.

Back in 1996, the town first became known for a terrible accident. An express train derailed, killing four people. At least 75 other people were injured, some of them seriously. At the time, it took the city a long time to recover from this event. No one suspected at that time that this accident would not remain the only one and that the small town was already facing a worse catastrophe at that time. A catastrophe that would put the small town back on the front pages of all Scandinavian newspapers just 11 years later.

Among the nearly 6,000 residents is Pekka Eric Auvinen, who is 18 years old in 2007. He lives in a small house in Jokela, together with his mother Mikaela Vuorio and his father Ismo Auvinen, who earns his living as a musician. Pekka Eric owes his name to his father's two favorite guitarists: Pekka Kiviaho and Eric Clapton.

This Wednesday, November 7, 2007, begins quite normally for everyone. The residents of the small town get up, shower, have breakfast and say goodbye to their loved ones before heading to work or school. While most people are thinking about what they're going to have for dinner that day or what appointments they have left in the afternoon, Pekka Eric has something completely different on his mind.

Today is the day he will put his plan into action. He has been longing for it for too long. That's why he didn't want to leave anything to chance and has planned and thought everything through carefully. He knows how he wants to proceed in the next few hours. Nothing can stop him now and no one has any idea what the 18-year-old is up to.

Around 11:40 a.m., he enters the school building. He has already missed the first lesson. In Finland, school doesn't start until around 9 a.m., but classes continue into the afternoon.

But today Pekka is not here to study. Today he has Cathrine with him. That's what he has named his semi-automatic Sig Sauer 22-caliber pistol. Semi-automatic means that the pistol reloads itself and is thus ready to fire again immediately after a shot or just with a slight delay. When faced with such a weapon, there is hardly any time to react.

Right after Pekka Eric enters the school building, he shoots 17-year-old student Sameli Nurmi in the school's entrance hall without a warning. The blast is a sudden one that is to kick off 24 deadly minutes.

At the same time, school nurse Sirkka Kaarakka is in the restrooms. As she washes her hands and thinks about what else is in store for that Wednesday, she gets a fright. Was that a gunshot just now? She pauses but can't detect any other sounds at first. She waves it off and almost laughs at herself. She's probably seen too many action movies. After all, she is in a school in safe Finland and not in a war zone.

But there are screams? Right in the next room. Now she can hear the shots clearly. One, the second, the third. Then silence. Sirkka's blood freezes in her veins. What is happening? She has to see if anyone needs help, opens the door and can't believe her eyes. Students covered in blood are lying on the floor. She quickly grabs her cell phone, dials 911 and yells to the other students who are in the hallway to run and hide. More shots are fired. Then, all of a sudden, he's standing in front of her. She knows him, because he himself is a student of this school. All attempts to appease him are unsuccessful. Pekka Eric shoots the 41-year-old woman in cold blood and without batting an eye at close range.

The rampage killer is full of adrenaline. His plan seems to be working. While the nurse was making the emergency call, the 18-year-old had already shot four other panicked students on their way to escape. They, too, had no chance to escape.

A student at the school is able to let a staff member know, who immediately contacts the principal, Helene Kalmi. She then places another emergency call and warns the approximately 50 teachers and 500 students over the building complex's public address system. She asks everyone to run to the classrooms and barricade themselves inside.

The fact that there are now no people in the hallways, and he cannot get into the rooms frustrates Pekka Eric. He fires 53 shots into the corridors of the school building, but they don't hit anyone.

Then suddenly the mother of a student meets him in the hallways. The unsuspecting woman is face to face with death. At first, he wants to shoot her, but then surprisingly turns away from her at the last moment.

After not having the desired success on the first floor, Pekka now decides to go to the second floor. Two students are wandering the corridors there in search of shelter; they haven't made it into the barricaded classrooms in time. When Pekka Eric discovers them, the gunman immediately shoots them as well.

Since afterwards he is confronted only with more locked doors on the second floor as well, Pekka purposefully hurries to the cafeteria. There, other students have barricaded themselves in. The crazed attacker tries to get in, but in the end has to abandon the plan. The students' self-made door lock holds too well.

Pekka Eric does not seem to have expected so much resistance. He leaves the interior and looks for more victims in the courtyard of the school complex. Principal Kalmi is there at the same time - she had given up her cover in the office to receive the rescue workers. The two run into each other. Death-defyingly, Helena Kalmi tries to placate the young man and get him to put down his gun. But Pekka Eric does not let her talk to him. With seven shots to the head, he kills the defenseless 61-year-old woman. She dies before the rescue services arrive.

Completely enraged, Pekka then makes his way back to the second floor of the school building. Once there, he begins to douse the floor with gasoline, but fails in his attempt to ignite the liquid with matches.

After all the doors are locked, Pekka Eric tries to gain access to the classrooms by knocking on them - in one room he actually succeeds. Frightened eyes look at him. Pekka starts a speech, talks about a revolt and asks the intimidated students to demolish the school facilities. He himself fires his pistol at the windows and the television set located in the room. Miraculously, however, he spares the students.

As the scenes unfold inside the school building, the police and rescue workers arrive at the school's courtyard. They first try to make contact with the 18-year-old spree killer. They do not get an answer. Instead, the shooter fires wildly, but fortunately does not injure anyone.

Just 24 minutes after he has started his revenge campaign through the school, Pekka Eric is on his way to the toilet room again, because the end of his crime is also exactly planned.

In the anteroom he takes off his jacket and bag, lays the things neatly together on the floor next to him, and executes himself at 12:04 with a shot to the head.

When the special task force first evacuates the completely frightened students, they also find the seriously injured Pekka Eric Auvinen in the toilet rooms. He is immediately taken to the nearest hospital. They want to clarify the circumstances and get the question of why answered by the perpetrator. But Pekka's head injury is too severe, and he succumbs to his injuries a few hours after arriving at the hospital.

Pekka Eric Auvinen is inside the school for exactly 24 minutes. 24 minutes in which he murders eight innocent people. Those minutes must have felt like hours to everyone involved. He fired 75 shots. On the bathroom floor, investigators recover magazines containing a total of 328 rounds.

Five students between the ages of 16 and 18, a 25-year-old who was completing her high school diploma, the 43-year-old school nurse and the 61-year-old principal; these are the victims of the Jokela rampage.

Within hours, the news spreads beyond Finland's borders. But not only the city, but the whole world must first come to terms with what happened. The question of why quickly arises. Since the perpetrator has evaded responsibility by committing suicide, he can no longer be questioned about it. For this reason, the investigative work is of immense importance.

The police officers get straight to work. In the weeks that follow, they search through and analyze Pekka Eric's entire life. They quickly discover his YouTube channel, where he had uploaded several videos. In most of the videos, the teenager films himself shooting at various objects.

In his YouTube videos, Pekka repeatedly explains his fascination with another school massacre - the rampage at Columbine High School on April 20, 1999, in Littleton, Colorado, USA. Two teenagers killed 12 students and a teacher. To this day, it is not known whether the crime was racially motivated. One of the perpetrators was considered a right-wing radical, and April 20 is also the date of Adolf Hitler's birth.

In any case, Pekka Eric admires the organizational spirit with which the two teenagers commit their crime and uses it as a template for his project. He, too, wants to cause the maximum possible damage in the shortest possible time.

In various Internet forums, he describes himself as a cynical existentialist. There he writes page-long texts describing his opinion of other people and his view of the world. Everything under the code name "Natural Selector 89".

This name has its own thoughtful meaning. "Natural Selector" refers to the founder of the theory of evolution Charles Darwin and his book "Origin of Species". According to this, animal and plant species have evolved according to the principle of natural selection. In this process, the best-adapted individuals survive. The stronger therefore prevails, the weaker dies. Pekka Eric despised weaker individuals and considered the majority of humanity to be extremely worthless in principle. The 89 stands for the year of birth of the spree killer.

While the police are pressing ahead with the investigation, the people of Jokela are still in a state of shock. They are all asking themselves the same question: Why? How could it have come to this? Why couldn't anyone see the signs that were abundant? Moreover, after it becomes known to the public that Pekka Eric had a fascination with the Columbine High perpetrators, the question even germinates as to whether murder is contagious.

Meanwhile, investigators delve deeper and deeper into the life of Pekka Eric Auvinen, reconstructing the days leading up to his crime.

A month before the murders, the young man applied for a gun license as a marksman for a sport shooting club and was approved. Five days before his rampage, the 18-year-old bought the pistol with which he shot his victims.

Originally, Pekka Eric wanted to carry out his plan with a 9 mm Glock, one of the most powerful handguns on the market. However, since all gun purchases in Finland must be pre-approved by the police, and the authorities refused to allow Auvinen to purchase such a large weapon due to his age, he had to switch to a smaller caliber weapon.

The investigations also show that the later shooter repeatedly made violence-glorifying as well as racist insinuations in various Internet groups before his crime. He stated that he wanted to fight for "his cause" and emphasized his willingness to die for his convictions. Pekka predicted his suicide and stated that he wanted to eliminate anyone he felt was too weak or considered a failure. These people would fall victim to natural selection anyway - the natural selection he saw himself as.

No one took his descriptions seriously or reckoned at the time that the 18-year-old's rampage would go down as one of the worst acts in Finnish history.

But who was Pekka Eric Auvinen really and how did he become this person?

At first glance, there is nothing remarkable about the Auvinen family. Both his parents and Pekka Eric himself were much involved with literature and music. There are no signs that Pekka Eric was brought up in a loveless home or with violence. On the contrary, his parents had always tried to make everything possible for him and supported him wherever they could.

Born on June 4, 1989, Pekka has a special personality even in elementary school. He often wears suits and uses a briefcase instead of a school bag. Although he is very talented, he is also insecure and extremely shy. He blushes easily and does not have a particularly good standing with his classmates. It is not long before he becomes a victim of bullying and can hardly stand life at school.

Pekka opens up to his parents, who take the situation very seriously. They immediately talk to the school administration. But the school neither responds to the accusations nor does it do anything to support Pekka. The boy and his parents are left completely alone with the problem. Helplessly, Pekka's parents have to watch their child suffer. He also withdraws more and more from his private surroundings and increasingly becomes a loner.

The older Pekka gets, the more his contempt for his peers increases. Although the teenager has some friends, he is massively bullied and ostracized until high school. He develops social phobias and suffers from panic attacks, for which his family doctor prescribes him antidepressants. He is allowed to request the prescriptions by phone. Perhaps that's why the doctor couldn't assess the teenager's mental state in more detail or check how the adolescent is doing and what hardships he's going through.

Once again it is Pekka Eric's parents who are not unaware of their child's suffering, and once again they try to get what they see as urgently needed help for their son. In early 2007, the Auvinens turn to a child and adolescent psychiatric clinic. They have long been aware that the tablets are no longer enough. But here, too, they are faced with closed doors - Pekka Eric's symptoms are too mild. No one wants to help them with their request and once again the family is left alone with their worries and problems.

On their own, the family then tries to find a psychologist who can help Pekka. However, the waiting lists are so long that appointments can only be made in the distant future.

No one seems to realize how acute the adolescent's problems already are and what plans he is making inside.

Father and mother watch as their son withdraws further and further and spends his time almost exclusively alone at home in front of the computer. Here he hangs out in Internet forums, researches various topics, shoots his YouTube videos or plays first-person shooters.

It was while playing one of these games that Pekka Eric met his first girlfriend. The two fall in love with each other. It is an Internet love affair that takes place exclusively in the virtual world; the two never meet in real life. Nevertheless, at first it seems as if Pekka's situation is becoming more stable thanks to his girlfriend. But after she breaks up with him and even mocks and humiliates him in public on the Internet, his condition worsens from day to day.

From now on, other students and the school's social worker notice that Pekka's behavior is getting drastically worse. He becomes increasingly aggressive and cynical, conveying to others his - consistently negative - opinion of society and humanity without mincing words. He speaks of a "white revolution" and glorifies violent extremists.

It so happens that the principal is also informed about Pekka Eric's behavior. However, since the young man is already of age at this point, his parents do not find out about the content of the conversation and their son's change of character.

Shortly before the crime, Pekka Eric increasingly displays his strong interest in politics and fascism. He names Hitler and Stalin as his greatest role models and thinks about emigrating to North Korea in front of his friends. Then, in one of his latest YouTube videos, he says he's had enough and is ready to die for a cause he knows is right and just. He would rather die fighting than live a long unhappy life.

Now that all the facts are out in the open, many people are questioning whether the crime could have been prevented had the various agencies Pekka's parents approached addressed the issues. The fact that the perpetrator is also a victim in this regard makes the whole case even more tragic. Perhaps the help Pekka and his parents sought could have saved not only their son's life, but also that of his victims.

Less than a year after this rampage, another young man causes a school massacre in Finland. He kills nine students and a teacher and injures another ten people. For his crime, he uses a firearm and Molotov cocktails. Afterwards, he also turns the gun on himself to commit suicide by shooting himself in the face.

Sadly, there are numerous similarities not only in death, but also in life between Pekka Eric and Matti Juhani Saari. Later it will become clear that Matti was also bullied and treated as an outsider during his school career. And he too admired the school massacre at Columbine High School in the U.S. and took it as a model in planning his own act, just like 18-year-old Pekka Eric Auvinen. After all, both left notes about how little they thought of humanity, and both suffered from mental illness.

The fact that private gun ownership is considered normal - sometimes due to hunting by private individuals, which is common in Finland - is considered a serious problem. Any person over the age of 18 can apply for a gun permit. It is not even necessary to have the appropriate training or proof of a marksman's license.

In the nine months between the two rampages, Finland has had 86 serious threats of school shootings. This is why the gun law is reviewed and tightened after Matti Juhani Saari's crime.

After the two tragedies, the commission decides to raise the minimum age for gun ownership from 18 to 20. In addition, anyone applying for a gun permit must have been a member of a shooting association for at least 2 years. Pekka Eric had registered in the shooting club in August before his crime. According to the people in charge, he attended a single practice session in the following months and got his license in October.

The rampage has sensitized not only politicians but also the authorities and agencies to which people seeking help turn to take their concerns more seriously. Teachers and students have been trained in bullying, because what can happen otherwise is brutally demonstrated by the case of Pekka Eric Auvinen. Finland's stricter weapons law came into force in 2008 - a few days after Matti Juhani Saari's crime. Since then, there have been threats, but no more shootings or rampages.

For the relatives of the victims, however, there will always be an empty chair at the dinner table. This is also the case for the parents of Pekka Eric Auvinen, who not only miss their son, but also have to come to terms with the consequences of his deed and the questions it raises. Should they have done more - or could they? All of Finland - and especially the homey little town of Jokela - will never forget the brutal act of November 7, 2007.

CHAPTER 10

Princess

on't be sad, Mommy. I can do it," says the blonde eight-year-old, comforting her worried mother. The little girl tries her best to radiate confidence all over her chubby face. Although she is still a child, she instinctively knows how frightening this moment must be for her mother. Because earlier, Eerika had delivered a terrible message to her mom that cut deep into both of their hearts: "I'm never coming home again." Her dad and stepmother told the little girl that she would never be allowed to see her mother again in the future.

A cruel moment, but what both do not suspect: This announcement is only the start of something even more terrible.

The brave little girl, Eerika Heleen Tarkki, was born on April 6, 2004, in Helsinki, and more precisely in the Mellunmäki district. She is born into difficult circumstances.

Her parents' marriage is already broken. Her father Touko beats his wife and is also charged with a sexual offense during this time. Four months after the birth of their child, the parents separate.

The period following the divorce is obviously difficult for the young mother, who increasingly tries to drown her sorrows in alcohol. At first, presumably so discreetly that it is not too noticeable, but in 2010 the problems become obvious. The alcohol addiction has now reached such proportions that Eerika's mother can no longer reliably care for her beloved daughter. The alarmed welfare department therefore decides that something must be done as a matter of urgency. She sees the child's well-being at risk. But since there are no suitable foster homes or places in orphanages available at this time, the six-year-old is placed in the care of her father Touko and his new wife. He is given custody of his daughter.

At this time, Eerika is described as a happy, bright and intelligent child who is very creative and loves to move around. In photos from this time, a happy girl with bright eyes looks out at you, who still has some baby fat on her ribs. The blonde hair is tied into cute braids that sit on the side of her head like that of Pippi Longstocking. The sociable girl sings in a children's choir and is absolutely infatuated with her rabbit, which she lovingly cares for. Her biggest dream, however, is to be a princess. A princess with a glittering crown.

Perhaps she has seen and heard many stories about princesses at this time when her young life is about to change decisively. Stories in which the girls have to bravely overcome countless dangers so that in the end they get the prince. Perhaps it is these tales, dream worlds, in which she seeks refuge after moving in with her father. Because Eerika will need all her imagination and strength for the challenges in the coming two years. Challenges that exceed human strength; but no one suspects that at this point.

Touko Tarkki, Eerika's father, is living with his new wife in a one-room apartment in the Puotila district of Helsinki. In fact, the studio is much too small for the three of them to live there in the future. But the welfare service has no alternative for the six-year-old and the father promises to look for a larger apartment as soon as possible. So Eerika moves in with him.

His new wife, Nadia Berough, takes care of little Eerika from now on together with Touko. The two have known each other for several years and Touko loves the brain surgeon of French-Moroccan descent, who has already practiced in Nice, France, among other places. Since she has already been pregnant four times in her last relationship, as Nadia explains, the staff of the Youth Welfare Office are convinced that Eerika will fare better here than with her drug-addicted mother. However, neighbors learn from Nadia that she is suffering from a brain tumor and is therefore being treated with strong medication by Touko. Rumors are also spreading that Eerika's father is also using Nadia's morphine. To neighbors and acquaintances, it occasionally seems as if Touko is on drugs.

At meetings, Tarkki repeatedly speaks in a slurred manner and makes a disoriented impression on them.

It was the declared wish of the biological mother to give her little daughter the name Eerika. For six years and two months the girl was also called that, during the good times when she was happy and felt loved - despite the difficult circumstances with her alcoholic mother. But when Eerika moves in with Touko and Nadia, many things change for the little girl. Even her name. From now on, she is addressed as Vilja. The reasons for this are not known: Perhaps the father had such a strong dislike for his ex-wife or Nadia simply did not like the name Eerika.

Living together in such a small space is problematic. Although Touko Tarkki has promised to look for a new, larger apartment, nothing happens and the three have to come to terms with living in such a small space. Problems soon arise, especially Nadia complaining that Touko's daughter has not been brought up well by her mother. The girl must finally be shown limits. In this context, Nadia also alleges to several other people that Eerika has smeared the walls of the toilet with feces. Other people who know the child are completely irritated; the girl had never done anything like that before.

It repeatedly happens that concerned neighbors contact the welfare department. They notice that Touko, for example, goes to work in a karaoke bar at night and suspect that the little girl is home alone. When asked by the authorities, the father always comes up with plausible explanations that appease the social workers. For example, he claims that the girl is with her grandparents or that Nadia is taking care of her.

At this time, Eerika's biological mother also sees her daughter again and again - even if only rarely. Because the visiting appointments are often not kept, but downright turned down. It seems as if Touko and Nadia do everything to prevent Eerika and her mom from meeting without supervision. Several times the mother has to complain about missed appointments to the responsible authorities. She does not always find the desired support there.

In addition, Eerika's mother notices that her formerly rather sturdy, fun-loving and good-humored daughter is increasingly changing. At first, this is more of a feeling, but it becomes more intense with each encounter. Until, during a visit, she abruptly makes a discovery that deeply disturbs her. The mother is full of anticipation and overjoyed, as she is every time a meeting with her little Eerika takes place and is not canceled for flimsy reasons. She spreads her arms wide to hug her little girl tightly in greeting. But as the beaming child runs toward her, the woman is suddenly overcome by an intense feeling that something is not right. Feverishly, her eyes scan the girl nestled in her arms. Almost seeking protection. When the woman wants to stroke Eerika's blond hair to calm her down, she understands. Gently, she grabs a strand and lets it glide through her fingers. Yes, indeed, the hair has become noticeably thinner! Then the mother lovingly but firmly pushes her daughter arm's length away from her so that she can take a better look at her. And she makes another disturbing discovery: the bare scalp is showing through in several places. As if her little Eerika's hair had fallen out - or been pulled out, in clumps. What is going on here? With trembling fingers, the worried mother instinctively wants to examine Eerika's forehead. As she gently brushes up her child's blond bangs with her hand and wants to take a photo, something happens that makes the whole situation even worse: Eerika begins to scream in panic and does everything she can to fend off her mother. Almost hysterically, the little girl screams that this is forbidden! And when asked about it, she sobs again and again, "I'm not allowed to say!"

Her mother is stunned and completely unsettled. Faced with a worry that simply cannot be true, she doesn't know what to do. So, she lets her daughter go. When she receives a call from Nadia a short time later, her suspicions are aroused. Nadia emphatically forbids her to take photos of Eerika; otherwise, there will be consequences!

Immediately after Eerika's mother is forbidden to take photos, neighbors in Puotila observe something strange: three to five times a day, the small, buxom girl comes out of the house and begins to walk in circles in a free space. Incessantly. Until complete exhaustion, spurred on by Nadia, who controls the child from the one-room apartment. She yells at the child even then, threats her, and orders her to keep running when she is already crying from sheer desperation. These spectacles can last up to two hours each. The whole time little Eerika has to run as if her life were at stake. When neighbors cautiously ask them what is going on, they only get the answer that the child's excess weight is to be reduced. At first, the neighbors think that these actions come from the father, Touko Tarkki, but then a resident notices that Nadia is clearly the merciless controller here.

In the secret of the apartment, Eerika is force-fed soups or fruit porridge - until the girl vomits. But even then, the ordeal has no end. Several times in a row, the girl is forced to eat until she throws up. All the crying and struggling does not help the girl, food is stuffed into the child over and over again. Later, it emerges that Nadia and Touko even recorded this force-feeding on video. They show the little girl crying while her face is covered with dark berry soup. Things go on until she regurgitates the soup. By way of explanation, Tarkki and his partner will later state that Eerika had an eating disorder and they knew no other way out. How this is supposed to fit together with the running sessions, they will remain guilty of this answer. Is the fattening meant to cover up the weight loss from the running?

At this time, a neighbor also witnesses Eerika taking a pee next to the garbage containers in the early hours of the morning when she has to take out the household garbage. In addition, Nadia complains loudly several times that Eerika has deliberately broken things or cut clothes into small pieces. The girl also allegedly steals or hides keys. Nadia is outwardly completely sure of her stepdaughter's "offenses" and demands that Tarkki punish his daughter severely. So far, he had simply been too careless with her.

In 2011, things pick up even more speed. Eerika has her first day of school at the new school. The girl, who now calls herself Vilja, irritates classmates as well as teachers and those in charge with her appearance. The once sturdy and cheerful girl, who would so much like to be a princess, is now a completely neglected appearance. Her head is bald, and she is covered with bruises. Because Eerika seems quiet and depressed, she is shunned by her classmates. She only has one friend, a girl from the second grade.

In addition, the child is often late for class. Therefore, the teachers eventually contact her father. Tarkki, however, is not aware of any guilt and explains that he makes his daughter walk the approximately 3.3 kilometers to school in the morning if she is not well-behaved and dawdles once again. In his opinion, this is an appropriate punishment. By way of comparison, in Germany the permissible upper limit for a first-grader's walk to school is 1.7 kilometers. However, this is only the case if no busy roads have to be crossed.

In addition, Eerika is turning up at school with injuries more and more often. When teachers ask her about it, the girl simply replies: She doesn't know how it happened.

At the end of 2011, Eerika's mother finally takes action. She, too, has noticed the child's changes during the few - and if only supervised - brief meetings with her daughter. She writes an official complaint to those responsible at the Youth Welfare Office. In it, she expresses her concern that her ex-husband may be abusing Eerika. Furthermore, she asks that she be given custody of her daughter again, since she has her life under control again and can take care of the first-grader appropriately. This request is not granted, although the mother does not shy away from seeking court assistance. Tarkki wants to keep the custody and is also against the meetings of mother and child, which he has tried to prevent so far. He claims that the meetings are extremely stressful for the child, and that it takes days for the child to calm down and rejoin the family. The court refrains from questioning Eerika personally and follows the father's version. The child is to continue living under his care and visits to her mother must be avoided in the future to ensure the child's well-being.

A short time later, however, new developments occur: In November, Tarkki asserts to the youth welfare office that Eerika has developed numerous behavioral disorders. He asks for support and gets it from the Youth Welfare Office. His daughter is temporarily placed in a foster home - and almost immediately a miraculous change occurs! Suddenly she seems like a changed child, like a completely different child. She is cheerful, laughs a lot, is outgoing, a little whirlwind - and all the educators and also the other children immediately take Eerika into their hearts. Remarkably, during all these weeks in the home, no new injuries appear, moreover, the old ones heal and are no longer visible. It feels a bit as if the old Eerika were standing in front of you again.

During these few months, the girl sees her father and his partner only on weekends. Everything seems perfectly fine and harmonious. But when the time in the home finally comes to an end and Eerika is supposed to go back to her father completely, the situation escalates. The child refuses to move back to her father. No, she doesn't want to! She would rather stay in the home!

Yet none of the people in charge at the facility attaches any importance to the whole thing. Since the time period granted for her stay at the home has expired and the authorities have decreed accordingly, Eerika, despite her categorical refusal, has to move back to her father's one-room apartment in Puotila. Tarkki has not kept his promises to the Youth Welfare Office to find a larger place to live.

Within a very short time, little Eerika starts to feel worse again. Her mysterious injuries reappear and her appearance quickly resembles what it looked like before she went to the home - neglected and unkempt. At school, too, Eerika's behavior becomes increasingly conspicuous. She destroys at least three of her school satchels. Most recently, Eerika comes to school with a plastic bag because Touko and Nadias don't want to buy her a new satchel. Repeatedly, the girl tears her schoolbooks into tiny shreds or loses them. In addition, she arrives late or complains that she feels sick. In addition, injuries can be seen on her body several times, but when teachers ask Eerika about them, the only evasive answer is, "I don't know."

The walls of the small apartment in Puotila are so thin that the neighbors hear more of what is going on in there than they would like. They keep hearing the girl's screaming and crying, the foul insults Nadia keeps using to humiliate the little girl. Eerika is a cow, a whore or a fat ass. She would be much too fat to ever make friends. And once, probably during one of the forced feedings, Nadia Berough even yells, "If you don't eat, you'll regret it!"

In the spring of 2012, the violence against Eerika reaches a new, even more horrific level. By now, neighbors are getting word that the father is also repeatedly yelling at the eight-year-old. It's just the tip of the iceberg, because since mid-April Nadia has come up with a new "consequence" for the girl. From now on, because the child is so restless in the evenings and at night, she has to sleep with her hands tied and wrapped in foil. This way, she would no longer disturb Touko and Nadia during their evening relaxation.

Nadia dismisses Touko's initial concerns by claiming that this measure is common practice in clinics. She has experienced this several times as a doctor. Eerika's father trusts the woman at his side, perhaps out of convenience, perhaps out of fear. Later he will testify that he was also afraid of Nadia in several situations and therefore let her go.

Thus, from now on, the eight-year-old girl's hands are tied in the evenings and then she is wrapped in foil to form a motionless package. Even the smallest movements are completely impossible, not to mention getting up to go to the toilet. How must she have fared during the nights in the confinement, in the heat that arose in the plastic wrapping?

Four weeks later, on May 12, 2012, things take their terrible course. On this Saturday, Eerika is scheduled to visit her grandparents together with her father. But Touko comes alone. His parents may be surprised, but so far Touko has always been able to pull excuses out of his hat that sounded quite plausible in all situations, both to social workers and to his parents.

Meanwhile, the girl was alone at home with Nadia. What happened there that afternoon can no longer be reconstructed. The only fact is that Eerika's hands were already tied for the night when her father returned from the visit. That day Nadia had already tied the child's hands and feet together with tape, as she usually does. But today this does not seem to be enough for her. On top of that she gets cable ties and additionally ties Eerika with them. Around each wrist and each ankle comes a cable tie, these are in turn fixed together by two more cable ties. In total there are eight pieces. Then the girl is wrapped tightly in a sheet, a plastic sheet is placed around it as an additional layer. This is how the child is placed on the sofa to sleep.

That evening, Nadia and Touko want to watch a movie on TV in peace, but they keep feeling disturbed by the girl on the sofa. Especially when Eerika bumps her head against their bed frame. It is the moment when the situation gets completely out of control. To make the child finally shut up, Nadia hits Eerika several times in the stomach with her fist, she also hits the soles of her feet with a cable and orders the girl to finally lie still. Finally, tape is put over Eerika's mouth and nose to stop her from making a sound. In addition, Nadia and Touko pull both the sheet and the plastic tarp over the child's face, up to her hair. Perhaps to emphasize their demands for quiet, the stepmother then once again presses her knee into the child's belly, while the father sits on the child's legs.

Eventually they finally let up and continue watching TV before Nadia and Touko also go to sleep. It becomes a decidedly quiet night for them.

The day after, it is May 13 and Mother's Day, Nadia wakes up around four in the morning because her bladder is pressing. When the woman returns from the toilet, she briefly jiggles Eerika.

But the girl does not stir. Now Nadia pulls down the tarp and the sheet and looks into a completely blue child's face. Little Eerika is dead. Suffocated. After a death struggle that lasted for at least four to six hours.

During the investigation, Nadia Berough and Touko Tarkki repeatedly affirm to the police officers that they did not mean to kill the child. The death, they say, was a terrible accident. The father also states that he had no idea at all that the temperature in the tarp would rise so much. Similarly, Nadia, the woman who claims to be a doctor, states that she truly believed Eerika could get enough air through the exposed scalp. During the autopsy of the little girl's body, a total of 89 signs of abuse are found on the eight-year-old's body.

When the case becomes public after the arrest of the two suspects, it is a shock that shakes the whole of Finland permanently. Immediately questions arise: How could this have happened in the first place? Why didn't the authorities act? Because it quickly becomes clear that there were more than enough tips to the Youth Welfare Office that were not acted upon. In addition to the mother, numerous neighbors in Puotila as well as the director of the elementary school have contacted the responsible authorities several times. However, a thorough investigation of the allegations and signs of child abuse failed to materialize. It also becomes clear that important contact points and authorities have not been sufficiently networked in Finland so far and that crucial information has simply not been passed on. The pediatrician in charge, for example, was surprised by the bruise on Eerika's face during a visit, but since she had no idea about the running, the cramped quarters with her father or the other clues, further steps were unfortunately not taken. Could Eerika's life have been saved? In light of the fact that in 2012 each social worker in Finland was responsible for about 160 cases, this is indeed questionable. Recommended in a study a year later were 20 to 50 cases.

However, the fatal inaction in this case is only a reflection of a frightening situation in Finland at that time. Between 2003 and 2012, about ten infants and children died each year as a result of domestic violence. About 300 were seriously injured during this period. These are the known cases; the number of unreported cases is higher.

The trial in the Eerika Heleen Tarkki case begins on August 30, 2012, in Helsinki. The two defendants, Nadia Berough and Touko Tarkki, are accused of abuse, deprivation of liberty and murder. Nadia is additionally accused of assuming a false identity.

The alleged doctor and neurosurgeon, a stocky woman with short, dark hair and a serious expression on her face, makes an almost maternal impression on many at first. Perhaps this is one of the reasons why, at the beginning of Eerika's ordeal, the mother, social workers and teachers assumed that the problems that arose were related to Touko Tarkki. However, it is becoming increasingly clear to attentive observers that Nadia is in fact playing a significant role in the incidents. A social worker who visits the apartment several times apparently has doubts early on with regard to the woman's real identity. This also applies to the stories she tells about her background. The man even asks Touko several times to send him information about Nadia's alleged four pregnancies, medical records, birth certificates or registration certificates of the children, school reports or something like that. However, despite being told that this would be delivered to his hand, the man does not receive any documents or proof of identity from Nadia. For this reason, the social worker even finally notes that Nadia, in his opinion, is not suitable as a caregiver for Eerika. The man considers the alleged doctor of French-Moroccan origin to be simply a liar. However, it does not occur to him that she also represents a concrete danger for Eerika.

Touko's family, on the other hand, takes a closer look. A sister-in-law working in the health care system inquired about Nadia in the health care facilities in Helsinki. The result of these inquiries is interesting and surprises those involved: the woman, who claims to be a doctor with foreign roots, is in fact a native Finn and had previously worked in a nursing home in Helsinki. However, she was kicked out there for stealing from a patient. Nadia's real name is Sirpa Laamanen.

As the proceedings continue, it becomes increasingly clear that Sirpa Laamanen is a highly problematic person. She left her first family because she suffered from severe mental health problems. She had not been taking her prescribed medication since 2007. Touko Tarkki claims that this is as unknown to him as Nadia's real name. His partner lied to him about her identity. During his explanations, Eerika's father also points out that he had always been afraid of Nadia or Sirpa. The abuse of Eerika had actually come from her.

The two defendants admit to having caused the death of the eight-year-old girl, but they plead not guilty to murder.

Due to the accusations and incidents in the room, the court orders a psychiatric examination of the two defendants to clarify their culpability. The result is unequivocal: both are fully culpable. The psychiatric experts are certain: both are completely capable of control and insight without any restrictions. Father and stepmother are capable of assessing the consequences of their actions.

The available evidence and the testimonies that draw the story of the little girl bring tears to the eyes of the judges and those present. They reveal a kaleidoscope of atrocities that have been repeatedly pointed out by a wide variety of people. Without the authorities intervening. The videos of force-feeding are also made the subject of evidence. They are documentations that exceed the limit of tolerability for some of those present in the hall.

At the trial, neighbors from Puotila confirm that 90 percent of Eerika's audible verbal attacks and abuse came from Sirpa, but the father was definitely involved as well. In this context, the prosecutor tells Tarkki that he can no longer hide behind his partner.

Another frightening moment in this criminal case is a key statement made by Sirpa. Although she herself overhears all the bad things and actions once again, she shows no remorse until the very end. One also searches in vain for compassion. Instead, she tells the court that she did nothing wrong. Everything that happened was done in agreement with Eerika's father. Yes, she had never even had anything against the child, it had only simply had to learn rules. The mother had failed here.

On March 19, 2013, the verdict in the case of Eerika Heleen Tarkki is issued. Her father, Touko Tarkki, and Sirpa Laamanen are both imprisoned for life.

The defense lawyers immediately appeal against the verdict, but the competent court of appeal upholds the first-instance decision. With regard to the role played by the father in the course of the abuse and killing, it is pointed out in the grounds that the father was obviously indifferent to the cruel treatment of his daughter. This is evidenced by the long period of time over which the incidents took place.

The appeal filed against the Court of Appeal's decision by the two perpetrators to the Supreme Court of Finland is dismissed directly without a hearing.

In the aftermath of this case, there was a public debate in Finland on how to improve child protection. In the course of this, several investigations were carried out, studies were made and working groups were also set up, for example in the Ministry of Health and Social Affairs. The latter suggested investing more financial resources in child protection. Furthermore, better sharing of relevant data should be ensured. So far, success seems to have been limited. According to police statistics, five to six children are still murdered in Finland every year.

While clearing out the apartment in Puotila, Touko Tarkki's relatives make a surprising discovery that sheds yet another telling light on the personality of the alleged Nadia. While clearing out the apartment, they discover at the very top of a shelf and in cupboards some keys and various items - things that Eerika is supposed to have stolen, hidden or lost. Sirpa Laamanen had used these items to justify her cruel punitive actions against the girl. However, the objects were so high up, so much out of reach of an eight-year-old child, that this allows only one conclusion: Sirpa hid them herself as a pretext.

None of this brings little Eerika back, who is buried in Vantaa, north of Helsinki. Her grave site bears the number 10-3-50 and in front of the eternal light that someone has placed in front of the tombstone, a princess tiara with lots of glitter and little feathers has been placed, just as Eerika particularly liked it.

In his remarks, the prosecutor had pointed out an important detail of the last hours of the little girl's life. When Eerika was found dead, she still had the little princess tiara on her head, which she had been given by her mother on her last birthday, a month earlier. By wrapping her head with the sheet and tarp, the small teeth of the hairband dug deep into the skin of her forehead. Four of the colorful glitter stones fell out. They are gone forever - like Eerika.

The prosecutor is sure Eerika was able to survive the horrors of the nights she was tied up and wrapped up because of that - because she sent her thoughts to the dream world.

There, where she was a princess. There, where the dreams of a little girl could still come true.

CHAPTER 11

Thou shalt not kill

Simon's brain needs a few seconds until it understands what is going on here. His body, however, reacts directly. His pupils narrow, his eyes fill with tears. His stomach contracts painfully and his heart seems to be beating so hard that it threatens to burst his little chest. He can't fall asleep because tomorrow is the math test he's so afraid of. But suddenly it's no longer the upcoming exam that keeps him awake, it's screams. Whimpering, desperate, sobbing words. "Stop it!" and "Please!" surge from the living room. As he curiously pokes his little head past the doorframe to get outside, a horrific scenario plays out before his eyes. His mom is lying on the floor. She is bleeding and crying. She shieldingly holds her arms in front of her face. Then a foot hits her. Her protective shield cannot withstand the kick. Her face is exposed. Simon's gaze wanders to the attacker. It is Dad. He pounds his fist relentlessly on the face that always smiles so lovingly at him. When he hears a creaking sound, as if something is breaking, Simon runs to his dad. He cries and begs him to stop, but he keeps going on and on, orders his son back to his bed and closes the door. Instinctively, Simon feels that he shouldn't contradict Dad.

Marko Tuominen sits at his desk and looks at his wristwatch. It's just after midnight. The Helsinki police station is still busy despite the late hour. He is not the only restless investigator whose cases give him no peace. It's easier to concentrate at night because no other colleagues or calls interrupt him. Only the familiar rustling of documents can be heard, the turning of pages in a folder and the scratching of ballpoint pens busily leaving notes in the files. But slowly Tuominen feels his fatigue taking over. He strokes his light hair and looks out the window right next to his seat. His face is only dimly reflected in the darkness. Nevertheless, the deep, dark circles under his eyes cannot be overlooked. Marko averts his gaze and tidies up some papers. Just as he takes the last sip of coffee from his cup, the phone rings. He almost swallows as the ringing breaks the nightly silence. He picks it up and speaks to a friendly colleague from dispatch, who transfers a call to him. A young man who wants to report a murder. Nothing unusual in the turbulent metropolis of Helsinki. But when Marko hangs up, he realizes that he won't be going home tonight.

The caller's name is Simon Junni, and he is 20 years old. Ten years ago, his father murdered his mother in their apartment. As a 10-year-old boy at the time, he had to witness everything. He still remembers the lukewarm night in August 1980 very clearly. Because a math test was due at school the next day, he lay awake in his bed. Then suddenly he heard the screams. His voice choked with tears as he described the details of the evening. The next morning, Simon saw his mother lying on the floor in the bathroom while he was brushing his teeth. After he returned home from school, his mother was gone. His father told him she was dead.

From the files from that time, Marko can see that such a case had indeed occurred in August 1980. The emergency services were called to an apartment building in Kontula, East Helsinki. Ismo Junni, then 37 years old, met the police officers at his apartment, where they found the naked body of his 36-year-old wife rolled up in a carpet. Ismo told them that his wife had drunk a lot the night before and then had taken a bath. While getting out of the bathtub, he said, she had an unfortunate fall and hit her head on the concrete of the tub. In the process, she had also lost one of her incisors. She died immediately. In the autopsy, the coroners confirmed the widower's story. The injuries on the body's head could have been caused by the aforementioned fall, and the woman did indeed have some alcohol in her blood when she died. Since there were also no signs of a violent altercation in the apartment, the case was categorized as an accident and archived.

Marko reflects. Hours have already passed since the call. Since then, he has been going through the files from that time. He tries to pay attention to every detail. Actually, the case is a closed matter and leaves no doubts. But the young man on the phone has described his version of the story so vividly that Marko is now very much in doubt. Simon Junni knows too many details for a hoax call intended to mislead the police. It is also easy to verify his identity. The reason he gives for not coming forward until now, ten years later, out of fear of his own father, is also extremely understandable. It must have been an indescribable trauma for the boy to see his own mother die and then to be dependent on the murderer for ten years as a child. Marko makes a decision: tomorrow he will resume the investigation of the Junni case.

After some sleep, the experienced investigator assembles a small team of colleagues the next day and presents the case to them. After everyone is up to date, the investigators start checking the identity of Simon Junni. In fact, he is the son of Ismo Junni. When Marko looks him in the ice-blue eyes, he is sure that the young man is telling the truth.

The interviews with relatives and neighbors reveal that Ismo visited her grave every day after his wife's death. No one doubts that the widower is grieving for his deceased wife. Nor has he met a new woman since then. However, a neighbor reported that she had noticed a change in Ismo's behavior. He constantly talked about death and dead people. The widower seemed to be fascinated by these topics. According to his neighbor, he even tried to get a job in a morgue - because he wanted to steal the gold teeth from the corpses. Ismo did not get the job. This statement makes Marko wonder, because his wife's corpse was also missing a tooth when it was brought to the coroner's office - a rather striking coincidence. But Marko does not believe in coincidences.

When Ismo sits across from him in the interrogation room, Marko doesn't notice anything peculiar. A man of medium height, medium stature, medium-fine hair in a shade between blond and brunette. Marko describes to him the suspicions against him. Ismo patiently lets him finish and does not interrupt him once. Then, to Marko's astonishment, he admits to the murder of his wife ten years ago. They had an argument, that's when it happened. He pulled out her incisor with pliers to see if she was dead or alive. After she showed no reaction, he knew she was dead. Ismo answers the question of what he did with her tooth by reaching into his jeans pocket. He pulls out his wallet and opens the small inner compartment, which can be closed with a tiny zipper. Marko feels nauseous as Ismo pulls out a yellowed incisor and places it on the table between them.

While Ismo is in custody, Marko goes through all the documents in the 1980 file again. The prompt confession strikes him as questionable; usually murderers deny their deeds outright. He doesn't have many clues, but the black and white photos from that time support Ismo's story. The tooth he has kept in his wallet for ten years is also strong evidence of his guilt.

The local media in Helsinki are abuzz with headlines about the new twists in the case. They call him the "Tooth Killer." Marko can't do anything with these sensationalist phrases. But the population jumps at it. Even the neighbor, who had told him about Ismo's desire to work in a morgue, contacts the inspector once again. Her husband, Matti, had died four years ago. He and Ismo were close friends. The case was closed as an accident. A fire in the cozy forest cabin in Herttoniemi, a suburb of Helsinki, caused by the heating stove. The rescue forces could do nothing more for Matti and the family dog. Both were found dead at the scene. As Marko reads through the 1986 file, he falters at one point. Matti's body was missing both incisors.

Again, Ismo calmly sits in front of him, again the inspector describes to him the suspicion of the crime. And again, Ismo immediately confesses that he killed his friend at the time, Matti, four years ago in his forest cabin. They had been drinking and Ismo could no longer stand Matti. He said his wife was beautiful and their marriage was enviable. Matti never tired of raving about it all - knowing that Ismo's wife had died only a few years before. Overcome by envy, he could no longer restrain himself. He hit Matti on the head with a glass vase from the windowsill. When he lay unconscious on the floor, he pulled out both of his incisors with a pair of pliers. He also picked them up in his wallet since then. He then set the shack on fire from the inside and outside with lamp oil and watched the fire from a safe distance.

When Marko returns to his desk, it is late. He remembers well the fire at Matti's cabin in 1986, because it was at that time that he had been promoted. Back then, in the 1980s, there had been a conspicuous number of fires in Herttoniemi. It is clear to the investigator what he has to do. During a sleepless night, he searches through all the files on the fires of that time. When the morning light falls softly through his window and the first colleagues from the early shift arrive, he makes a discovery. In two other cases, there are bodies that were also missing their incisors.

Two months before Matti's murder, Ismo meets Seppo and Juha on the beach at Herttoniemi. The two men are about his age and are sitting in the sand drinking beer and laughing. Ismo quickly strikes up a conversation with the two. They talk about the fires, there must be a firestarter going around about women and sports. When it gets dark, Seppo and Juha invite Ismo to come to their cabin in the forest. A few bottles of beer are kept cold there, and they can also find a bottle or two of vodka in one of the cupboards. Once inside the hut, they sit on wooden benches around the table. Ismo is burning with anger. The two have an enviable friendship. They constantly make little jokes that only the two of them understand. Every other sentence begins with "Remember when we ..." Ismo, on the other hand, has no one to call for a beer on the beach. No one with shared memories and his own familiar jokes. In the blink of an eye, he loses all desire for alcohol. Seppo and Juha, on the other hand, lie on the benches after another hour, drunk off their asses. Ismo grabs one of the candles that gave them light that evening. There is no electric light in the hut. He throws the burning candle on the floor, between the two sleeping men. Then he takes a tea towel and puts it on the hot stove. When it catches fire after a few minutes, Ismo leaves the hut. He stokes the fire with gasoline and thus sets the whole hut on fire. He drops the small canister on the ground while still on the scene.

The investigators of the time also classified this incident as an accident. After all, remains of the burnt tea towel were found on the stove. No one noticed the canister with the flammable liquid. Again, Ismo confesses immediately and again he tells the truth. Every detail matches the photos and descriptions in the file at the time. The canister can be seen on one of the photos exactly in the place Ismo recounts.

But even after this story, Ismo is not finished with his confession. Two years after the fire, in 1988, Ismo meets Pauli in Herttoniemi's small liquor store. The elderly man permanently lives in his hut in the forest as a hermit. Ismo accidentally steps on his foot in the cramped store and apologizes post-haste. The hermit responds kindly and the two quickly strike up a conversation. Pauli finally invites Ismo to his hut for a glass of wine. There the two spend a few hours together, talking animatedly. As Ismo gesticulates wildly while talking, he hits a porcelain figurine with one hand, which falls to the ground and breaks. Pauli doesn't own much. But what he does own has meaning and special value to him. So does this inherited porcelain figurine. Pauli gets angry and asks Ismo to leave. The latter leaves the hut but turns back halfway. Nobody is going to talk to him in such a disrespectful way. He waits. When he sees Pauli sleeping through the window a little later, he takes revenge. Using lamp oil, he first sets fire to the outside of the hut and then to the swing set that stands a little further away at the front of the property.

A photo in the investigation file and a corresponding note prove that the grass between the hut and the swing did not show the slightest burn marks, which suggests that the perpetrator set fire to the hut and the swing one after the other. Again, Ismo tells the truth.

In 1992, the trial of Ismo takes place in Helsinki. To everyone's surprise, he retracts all his confessions right at the beginning of the hearing. He affirms that at the time of the fires he was undergoing treatment in a closed facility. Ismo's testimony is nothing more than an unnecessary postponement of the conviction for the investigators. It is quickly discovered that Ismo was indeed in a medical facility for treatment at the time - but it was not locked. He may very well have been able to sneak out unnoticed in the late evening hours until the early morning. The defendant finally buckles and confesses to having done just that.

Ismo's psychiatric report paints a talkative, open man who easily strikes up conversations with new people. He is what one would initially call "good company" when spending an evening among friends over a few bottles of beer. However, this is exactly where Ismo's dark side shows. When he drinks, he quickly becomes aggressive. He can't handle jokes at his expense, let alone insults and arguments. Then a pronounced need for revenge awakens in him, which leads him to completely disproportionate actions. All the victims died from base motives. Ismo killed out of envy, because he felt attacked or provoked. In possession of his full presence of mind, he is both aware of his actions and their deadly consequences.

Ismo is sentenced to nine years in prison for the manslaughter of his wife, and later to six years for assault resulting in death. He receives life sentences for each of the arsons and the four murders of Matti, Seppo, Juha and Pauli.

Ismo serves just under four years of his sentence until he is admitted to the Helsinki hospital in 1995. At the age of 51, his heart no longer receives sufficient blood flow. Only a bypass operation can save his life. The surgeons do their best, but complications arise. Ismo Junni does not wake up from the general anaesthesia.

The name "Simon Junni" is invented. It is unknown what Ismo's son's real name is, where he lives and how he regards his father.

CHAPTER 12

God

His blood is dark red. Like streams in stormy weather, it shoots out of the wounds that Jarno had inflicted on him earlier with scissors. Three times he has rammed the sharp blades into his left side. He has tied him to the radiator with duct tape for his safety. His dog is large and has a firm bite. Never in years of living together has he made use of it, but Jarno knows: the survival instincts of any living creature are stronger than anything else. The animal makes unbearable sounds. It screams and whines in a tone that Jarno has never heard before. It gasps for breath. In its dark brown, large eyes, Jarno sees mortal fear, but also astonishment. The attack was completely unexpected for the dog. Smiling, Jarno reaches for the metal bar lying on the ground next to him. Without hesitation he hits the animal on the head three times. The whimpering stops abruptly. It is dead silent. Jarno drops the rod and looks at the lifeless animal, whose head is now only a grayish-blood-red, smeared mass. Jarno's throaty laugh breaks the silence. He has decided. He is his own god.

Tarje exhales heavily. Looking up, he gazes into the equally tense faces of his three friends and colleagues. The four young men are on a mission: they want to help alcoholic youths find the right path. For them, the right path is the path with God. As volunteers of the Pentecostal Church in Järvenpää, they regularly open the doors of the Christian institution for young people. Their fates touch Tarje deeply. The region north of Helsinki spreads a harmonious glow. The vast landscapes, lush green fields in summer and magical snowy landscapes in winter - no one is surprised that life satisfaction in Scandinavia is higher than anywhere else in the world. But this appearance is deceptive. For there are black spots in the idyll. Tarje gets to know exactly these, the lost people who cloud the statistics. Sexual abuse, violence and humiliation find their way through every shining landscape, through every layer of snow, no matter how high. They don't knock timidly, but smash doors, sometimes even entire walls. That's what it feels like for those affected. In alcohol, many find a quick and easy solution. A few sips that warm them from the inside and shield them on the outside from the reality they can no longer stand. Tarje and his colleagues meet the lost souls they encounter in their missionary work with trust and empathy. A few alcoholic youths actually join the Pentecostal church afterwards. They turned in time on their way after all and arrived that way. The encounters are not always as pleasant as in these cases. Most of the time, the missionaries do not hear from the visitors after the initial meeting. But never before has there been a meeting like today.

It is a typical Finnish Saturday evening in November. It has been raining and storming for days, and even on this November 21, 1998, the clouds hang low in the sky. At this time of the year it does not get light in Finland. The days are full of night. So Tarje and his colleagues do not notice how time passes. They sit in the tea room of the Pentecostal Church and review the day. The clock on the wall above the kettle shows 10 pm. Time to clean up and go home. As Tarje puts his teacup in the dishwasher, he hears loud voices. There are several of them. They sound slurred and they come closer. He looks around questioningly, but his colleagues also shrug their shoulders. Tarje takes heart and runs to the door. "Hello?" he calls, "Can we be of assistance?" A few moments later, the voices turn into faces. They belong to four young men and one woman. All wear their hair long, black and loose. It falls straggly into their pale faces. The woman's eyes are ice blue and outlined with thick, black eyeliner. Her lips are also painted pitch black. The only splashes of color are the lettering of the band's logos, which stand out from their dark shirts. Tarje is not familiar with any of these bands. But he sees from the typical lettering that they must be black metal groups. One of the men is a bit taller and stronger than the rest of the group. A long beard hangs down from his chin. It is he who answers Tarje, "We need to talk about your faith." Tarje hesitates. The four are obviously drunk. To that end, they clearly embody what is spreading fear and terror throughout the country right now: the "Satanic Panic." This refers to what is known as "moral anxiety" - a social phenomenon in which a social group is perceived by the public as dangerous to order and morality because of its behavior. Tarje's gaze falls back to the shirts of the visitors. He knows that many black metal bands spread satanic content in their songs. One of his colleagues clears his throat. Tarje can imagine that his friend is afraid. The atmosphere is strangely tense. He does not feel well either and would like to crawl home to his warm bed. But just at that moment he dismisses the thought again, because he remembers his faith and his mission. It is precisely these people who need his help the most. "Sit down," he therefore says, earning suspicious looks from his colleagues. The man with the long beard goes ahead and sits down on one of the wooden chairs. With his arms folded, he begins the conversation, "Christianity is the purest waste of time." Tarje swallows hard. Still, he lets him speak, even when the man quotes from the Church of Satan: "Satan represents pride, freedom and individualism. These are qualities often degraded as evil by those who worship external deities. We Satanists are our own gods. We are benevolent gods who give love to those who deserve it. And we make those who tempt us to do so feel our wrath." This is not easy for the Christian missionaries to hear. They quickly realize that they are getting nowhere with their argumentation. But to their positive surprise, the conversation is completely non-violent. Four of the guests sit quietly while the apparent leader of the group speaks. After about an hour, however, even he seems to realize that this conversation is going nowhere. The group leaves the Pentecostal church. Relieved, Tarje and his colleagues also make their way home a few minutes later.

"Fuck the Christians, fuck God, I am my own God!" proclaims Jarno Elg shortly after they leave the Pentecostal church. It should have been clear to him that he cannot change the minds of the ordinary missionaries. In his opinion, they are already too blinded by the Bible and the church. Who knows what the pastor drills into them on Sundays during the service. But the alcohol has made him talkative. At least now the guys know that there are other people who are not impressed by them. "Exactly!" his girlfriend Terhi agrees with him, "Nothing but foreign controlled they are. That's no kind of life." Jarno puts his arm around her. Who would have thought that he would find his soulmate already at the age of 23 - but in 17-year-old Terhi he recognizes exactly that. He's glad she's back. Just a few weeks ago, she was released from psychiatric treatment. She has been addicted to alcohol and mentally unstable since the ninth grade. In Jarno she now finds her support. Together with her three friends Mika, Lars and Till, they stagger to the train station in Järvenpää. But "friends" is not exactly the right word. Jarno met 20-year-old Mika during one of his stays in a psychiatric ward. Since then, the two have been inseparable. Already during the group therapy sessions, Jarno noticed that Mika also had the absolute urge and conviction to live a self-determined life - a life without regard for the legal system and social orders. Most people only exist. You can't call the everyday run in the hamster wheel "life". After a few conversations with Mika,

Jarno was able to convince him of Satanism. For him, it is the only true meaning of life. 23-year-old Till and 16-year-old Lars have not been part of the group for long, but they share his beliefs. Jarno knows that Till has no job and is as addicted to alcohol as he is. Sometimes, they also take drugs. Till no longer has any contact with his family and no friends. He is a typical outsider who has now found a connection in the Satanist group. All Jarno knows about Lars so far is that he dropped out of school and has no fixed abode. Whether his parents are dead or have simply abandoned their son, Lars has never said. Actually, Jarno doesn't care either. Anyway, everyone should rely only on themselves.

Shortly after midnight, Jarno, Terhi, Mika, Till and Lars arrive at Jarno's apartment in Hyvinkää. The host is thirsty. It is a thirst that has lasted for years and does not seem to dry up. He pounces on the open bottle sitting on the coffee table. Terhi comes up to him, she wants a drink too. Jarno hands her the bottle and his girlfriend takes a big sip of the "Kilju", a Finnish sugar wine. Mika, Till and Lars drink beer. Mika keeps looking intensely at Jarno as they do so. He remembers how they met. The two were in psychiatric treatment at the same time because of their alcohol addiction. While therapy once again did not help Mika, he found fulfillment in Jarno, who is three years older than him. For Mika, he is a born leader and an inspiration. He lives his life free from any conventions. His guiding principle is Satanism. It allows him to be his own god. Again and again, Mika hears this from Jarno's mouth, including this evening. Jarno has already announced before their trip to the city that he wants to play them the new album of "Ancient" tonight. The Norwegian black metal band has created a masterpiece with "The Chronicle of Cain", according to Jarno. The first notes resound, dark basses, distorted guitars to a rough voice. The five listen to the music together. In between, Jarno explains to the rest of the group that the lyrics are about the biblical story of Cain and Abel. Cain killed his brother in order to sacrifice him. He adds that the band uses the lyrics to make a reference to Satanism. Everyone listens to Jarno's fiery sermon with fascination. Mika notices the skull ring on one finger of the wildly gesticulating hand.

After an hour, the exuberant mood suddenly tips over. It's Till, slurring his words and yelling that he doesn't like the music. Terhi, Mika and Lars look at him, startled. Jarno's gaze darkens. Till violates two important rules of the "Eleven Satanic Principles" with his behavior. He ignores principle number one and three:

One:

Express your opinion or advice only when asked.

Three:

If you are in someone else's den, show him respect, or do not go there.

Immediately, the fourth principle appears in Jarno's mind's eye:

Four:

> *If a guest behaves inappropriately in your cave, meet him harshly and without mercy.*

Jarno makes a decision. He is his own god.

In four weeks, it will be Christmas. These are Malte's last thoughts as he makes his way to the Hyvinkää landfill on this November 24, 1998. His wife has asked him to dispose of the electrical waste. Every year, she starts her holiday preparations early and thoroughly cleans the house before putting up the Christmas decorations. Every year, some items have to leave the house, and every year it's Malte who does the disposal at the landfill. But this year, Malte doesn't throw the garbage bag into the dumpster with any momentum, and then makes his way back home. This year, he falters before disposing of the trash in the large container. At first, he thinks the object inside is part of a mannequin. But since when are a mannequin's legs covered in thick hair? Malte retches when he realizes that there is a severed human leg in front of him.

Shortly afterwards, the police rush directly to the place where it was found. The rest of the body is not in the garbage can. The case is immediately treated as a murder investigation, even though the officers have no experience in this direction - a murder has never happened in Hyvinkää.

Forensic experts examine the leg. It is a left leg that has been severed from the thigh. The cut is not a medical-professional one - it is uneven. Based on the hair on the leg, the medics assume that the victim is male and between 20 and 60 years old. However, nothing is certain at this point; the body part could also have belonged to a woman. In order to be able to determine the victim more closely, the leg alone is not sufficient. The investigation therefore focused on the search for other body parts.

The search operation of the following days puts the idyllic residential area of Hyvinkää into turmoil. Officers spend days at the landfill searching through mountains of waste. With their bare hands, they comb through every container, every sack and every cardboard box. The head of the investigation, Ari Soronen, calls in students from the police academy to help deal with the stinking piles of garbage. During the nights, Finnish soldiers stand guard to prevent unauthorized persons from gaining access to the site. Cadaver-sniffing dogs support the unsuccessful search. The officers, led by Ari Soronen, are desperate. It is their task to return to the residents of Hyvinkää their security, the feeling that was previously normality in the village.

After a long week of searching, one of the sniffer dogs strikes. The officers find a piece of unwrapped human abdominal tissue. Tissue analysis yields important findings that move the investigation forward decisively: The DNA from the abdominal tissue and the leg match. The victim is male, between 20 and 30 years old, and was heavily intoxicated at the time of his death. Deposits on the tissue suggest that the man was basically drinking heavily while alive. Investigators believe that the victim must have been living on the fringes of society and on welfare - not a single missing person report has been received to date. The dead man does not seem to be missing to anyone.

Ari Soronen's team has no experience with murder cases, but they get right on the right track. They learn from the welfare authorities that there is indeed a man who has not been cashing his welfare checks for days. The man in question is 23-year-old Till from Hyvinkää. The coroner's office was able to narrow down the time of death to last weekend. Till was seen together with a group on Saturday evening. The members of this group are described to investigators as unpleasant. Just like Till himself, they were probably Satanists. Till's neighbors consider the young man to be a loner and an outsider. He never actually leaves the house and never gets visitors. When the officers contact his parents, they reply unimpressed that they have had no regular contact with their son for years.

The investigation quickly leads the police officers to the Pentecostal church in Järvenpää. The young man they talk to introduces himself to them as Tarje. He is a Christian missionary who helps fight alcohol addiction among local youth. When the investigators show him a photo of Till, Tarje confirms that he was at the church with four other young people last Saturday night. He reports the conversation and the group's affiliation with Satanism, but also that Till himself said nothing. He says that only one of the men spoke, a tall, burly one with a goatee. The policemen thank Tarje and go to the scene of Satanism, which is popular among young people at that time. They are shocked when they get direct answers to their questions. Till has actually been murdered. His friends, led by one Jarno Elg, sacrificed him to Satan. The deed was the ultimate confession for Jarno, a proof of loyalty for his followers to Satanism. That is why he has been proudly telling about it in the scene for days.

On December 08, 1998, the investigators arrest Jarno, Terhi, Mika and Lars. They find Till's DNA everywhere in Jarno's apartment - on the floor, on the walls and on the ceiling. If they didn't know about the case, they would have assumed from the sheer amount of blood that several people had died here.

Sitting in front of Ari Soronen are young people who have clearly lost their way. They are alcoholics, some of them drug addicts, unemployed and rebelling against law and order. But the investigator also notices that all three are intelligent. All the more terrible and serious is what he learns in the course of the questioning.

A fight has broken out. Till did not adhere to the principles and was disrespectful. He criticized the music and, worse, did not understand the deeper meaning in it. Jarno hit him, whereupon Till became even more quick-tempered. At Jarno's command, Mika and Lars then put a studded belt around his neck. Till had to crawl on all fours in front of the group like a dog. At the word "dog," Jarno laughs and recounts, as if it were an anecdote, that he had sacrificed his pet in a similar fashion a month earlier. Ari Soronen does not interrupt him once. He is deeply shocked but has studied the subject of Satanism. He knows about the eleven principles, which is why the tenth occurs to him at this point in the narrative.

Ten:

> *Do not kill non-human animals unless they attack you or you need them for food.*

Ari Soronen focuses on Jarno again as he continues with his narration. Mika, Lars and he took turns urinating on Till. They had drunk a lot of alcohol, the urge to urinate was great. All four, including Terhi, hit him several times. A hot iron bar was also used. At some point Jarno was disturbed by Till's screaming, whereupon he hit him on the head with a pair of scissors. Till lost consciousness. Meanwhile, at Jarno's request, Mika and Lars closed the unconscious man's mouth with tape. But apparently this task was too difficult for them, because the tape slipped. When he regained consciousness, Till pleaded for his life and promised that he would not tell anyone about what had happened if they let him go now. Again, Jarno laughs and describes Till as a coward. This time Mika and Lars got it right and wrapped Till's entire head with duct tape. Ari Soronen gulps. Till could no longer breathe and suffocated. After his death, Jarno cut out Till's heart and intestines. He smiles while he talks about it and points with his hands to his belly for illustration. After that, they cut off the corpse's penis. The ceremony also included eating parts of the victim. Using a knife, they cut the flesh from the dead body and ate it raw.

When they were done, they decapitated the victim and played with the severed head, throwing it to each other like a ball. It wasn't until late that night that Mika and Lars left the scene. When Jarno and Terhi woke up the next morning, they didn't remember where they had put the head. Finally, Terhi found it in a closet. To get rid of what was left of the body, they moved the remains to the bathroom and sawed them into pieces, which they stuffed into garbage bags and disposed of in various trash cans around town.

Jarno recounts the events of Saturday night to Ari Soronen not only willingly, but with pride in his voice. Quite the opposite of his girlfriend. Terhi affirms that they never intended to kill Till. They had all been drunk and unaware that he would suffocate from the tape on his mouth and nose. When they finally realized that Till was dead, they had to do something. Cutting up the body seemed like the easiest solution. Mika testifies that he was under the influence of alcohol and had merely followed Jarno's orders. He had not eaten any of the body parts, he had only hit Till a few times before that. The 16-year-old Lars states that he was forced by the others to take part in the crime. Out of fear, he participated, but left the apartment before the body was dismembered.

Jarno, Terhi and Mika remain in custody until the trial begins. For Lars, a conviction is out of the question because he is a minor. He is sent directly to a closed psychiatric ward.

Jarno's psychological report shows that he is fully conscious and has acted knowingly.

The trial begins in August 1999. At the request of the lawyers, the proceedings take place in camera - journalists and reporters are only allowed to be present during the first hour. As Jarno enters the courtroom, silence falls in the pews. The terrible deed is firmly anchored in everyone's memory; everyone has their own images in their head. He wears his hair and beard unchanged. For his clothing, he has chosen a band shirt and a red plaid, loose-fitting shirt. With his head held high, he sits down. He grins. Whenever he notices that a camera is pointed at him, he shows his middle finger or the "heavy metal salute" with raised index and little finger. Terhi has her black hair tied up tightly and wears no makeup. She has not been together with Jarno for some time.

The court decides that the case should be subject to a reporting ban. Only 40 years later, in 2038, may details about the investigation, the trial and the victim be revealed. At this point, in the midst of the "Satanic Panic," the court does not want to alienate the public. Besides, the danger for copycat offenders would be too high. However, the sentences will be announced to the public on August 11, 1999. Mika is sentenced to two years and eight months in prison for accessory to murder and desecration of corpses. Terhi gets 8 years and 6 months as an accomplice and Jarno's sentence as the mastermind is life in prison.

Mika is the only one of the three perpetrators to have served his entire sentence. Since his release, he has had no criminal record apart from drunk driving.

Terhi was released in 2003, after four years in prison. In 2007, she commits another murder. She kills an acquaintance in an argument with a garden knife. Since more than three years had passed without a crime before, she was considered a first offender under Finnish law at the time and received only half the sentence. In prison, she meets a murderer and falls in love with him. After her release in 2017, they move to northern Finland and start a family.

"Death is rebirth. The end brings new beginning. Ever turning the wheel of the Pagan cycle - Death is rebirth. The end brings new beginning, Ever turning the wheel of the Pagan cycle," reads one of the songs from "The Cainian Chronicle." Jarno was released on parole in 2016. Today, he is a free man. He has caught up on his schooling and works full time. Where he lives, what his personal life is like, and whether he continues to identify with these song lyrics is unknown.

Note: Due to the reporting ban, the victim's name has never been disclosed. "Till" is a fictitious name.

CHAPTER 13

In front of a closed door

"The democracy and unity of our society are supporting values based not on the equality of all - but on respect for the humanity and mind of every other individual.

- Sauli Niinistö, 12th president of the Republic of Finland

Li Andersson takes a big gulp of water as the first audience members enter the spacious meeting room of the Jyväskylä City Library. As chairwoman of the "Left Youth," she is used to speaking in front of people, presenting her ideas and addressing critical questions. She owes her outward composure to this habit. The young woman is on fire for her job, which revolves around her ideas of values and justice in a modern world. This passion is paying off - at just 24, she was elected chairwoman of the Left Youth. But speaking in front of large crowds still triggers unfounded stage fright in her. "Are you all right?" she hears Mikael Brunila ask.

The young man is a journalist and activist for social issues and environmental protection. "Yes, thank you," Li replies, smiling. She is glad to have Mikael by her side today. The young man is tall, slim and almost always wears a cap over his tousled, dark blond hair. He radiates security and calm, which also transfers to Li. She brushes a blond strand behind her ear and looks at the book lying on the lectern - her book. It is entitled "The Extreme Right in Finland." Li wrote it together with Mikael. The third author, Dan Koivulaakso is not present today. As a city councilor for the Left Alliance in Helsinki, his schedule does not allow for a book presentation at the public library. But he knows he can rely on Li and Mikael. The topic of right-wing radicalism in Finland is more topical than ever. The "Nordic Resistance Movement" spreads radical right-wing ideas throughout Scandinavia and captivates a large part of the youth with populist slogans. In addition, the branch of the "Finnish Resistance Movement" is up to mischief in Finland. They recognize white people as a superior race and fight for traditional role and family images. Adolf Hitler is a role model for them. For Li, Mikael and Dan, it is a matter of the heart to educate society about this movement and its dangers. Their book was recently published and today, January 30, 2013, Li and Mikael are presenting it at the public library in Jyväskylä, a university town 300 kilometers north of Helsinki. On the way to the event, the two were still talking about a right-wing extremist incident a few months ago, there was no way around it. Because the tragedy that happened just a few towns away is directly related to today's event. On July

19, 2012, a fellow activist was speaking at an LGBTQ parade about violence against minorities when a young man literally jumped on him and sprayed pepper spray in his face at close range. While the speaker was writhing in pain, the perpetrator aimed his spray bottle at the crowd and pulled the trigger. Twenty innocent people were injured. The man used the seconds of utter horror on parade to disappear unnoticed. Li, Mikael and Dan were horrified by the physical violence and the attack against freedom of political expression. As authors who clearly speak out against right-wing extremist terror, they too had already experienced hostility. So far, however, these have been limited to the online world. When they announced their book on Facebook, they were met with resentment, rejection and insults. One of the users even calls the book a betrayal of the state. Mikael, Li and Dan agree: this hatred is just one more reason to get their book out to the people and prevent worse things from happening by educating them. Nevertheless, the police have been informed before the book launch and bouncers have been organized - nothing stands in the way of a safe event.

Only a few minutes left until 6 p.m., the start of the event. During the day, the sun has shown itself, which is a real rarity at this time of year. The warm, bright rays have lured many people out of their homes on this winter day. Many of them are also drawn to Li and Mikael's event. By now, about 200 people occupy the hall, and the doors are closed. There is no longer any sign of the sun's rays, now glaring neon lights flood the audience. A spotlight is directed at Li and Mikael. "Good evening, I'm glad to see so many of you here tonight," Li opens the event. After a few sentences, she is in her element. Mikael and she explain the need for her book and its contents. The guests listen intently. In between, the authors involve them, ask questions and get talking. The beginning of the evening is a complete success - until screams are heard from outside and an attempt is made to break down the door by force.

Shortly after Li and Mikael have greeted the audience, Arno closes the door of the hall. He thinks about the pepper spray attack a few months ago and how crazy right-wing terror is. What kind of people are these who think patriarchally in this day and age, declare entire ethnic groups to be inferior, and are as critical of the European Union as they are of climate change? He has already accompanied many events and attended to the doors of many halls. As a doorman, he comes into contact with all kinds of people. But today's event interests him personally. He takes it upon himself to read the speakers' book. As he is about to sit down on the small chair to the right of the door, he hears a beeping sound coming from his belt. His radio makes itself heard. It's the receptionist at the public library. Three men have just entered the building, and they seem strange to him. One of them is wearing goggles, gloves and a bulletproof vest, the other is carrying a bag full of empty glass bottles, and the third is walking behind him with a digital camera. He said they are relatively young, of medium height and with strong builds.

He said he had already notified the police, but they would not come for now - the situation was not a clear danger. "Best keep an eye on the three anyway, I think they want to get into the hall," speculates the doorman - and he should be right. Arno sees the threesome from a distance. Without saying a word, they approach him with firm steps. "Good evening," Arno greets them in a calm, low voice, "the event has already begun. I'm afraid I can no longer let you in." Three pairs of dark eyes twinkle at him, but no one says a word. Seconds pass, and if Arno had a pair of scissors, he could cut the air. Suddenly he feels a pain in his face and takes a brief moment to realize what just happened. It was the fist of the man with the bulletproof vest that hit him quite abruptly. While Arno is still holding his cheek, one of his colleagues rushes toward the troublemakers. "Hands off the door!" he shouts. The three try to gain access to the hall, but they make no headway. Apparently, the startled onlookers from inside are holding out against them. "Pull yourself together," Arno meanwhile talks to himself for courage, still standing beside himself. He has never experienced such an escapade in his twenty-year career as a security guard. While his colleague tries in vain to talk to the three men, Arno contacts the doorman with his radio. "Call the police, those three are insane!"

More long minutes pass and there is no sign of the police. Arno hears the roar inside the hall through the massive wooden doors as the attackers continue to rattle the door. The onlookers seem to be getting scared, who knows how much longer they will manage to keep the door closed. Or what else the three men have in their luggage to gain entry by force. Arno hears his colleague inform the three about the police and how one of the men then attacks him with a glass bottle. He draws his baton and fights back. Without hesitation, Arno steps in to help. He grabs the chair that has fallen to the floor after the punch and throws it at the three young men. He hits them in their midst, but no one is hurt. Then everything happens very quickly. Arno's colleague falls to the ground and the three men suddenly run away. At first, the guard is surprised by the intruders' change of heart. Why, when they so urgently wanted to get into the hall, did they now flee? Have they perhaps heard the emergency call to the police? But then he realizes - his colleague is bleeding. One of the men has stabbed him in the upper body with a knife.

Arno answers all the questions put to him by the police, who arrive shortly afterwards. At the same time, his colleague is driven to the hospital. It later turns out that his injuries are not life-threatening. The attacker with the knife is quickly suspected of having committed the pepper spray attack in July 2012. The motive is therefore in all likelihood a right-wing extremist one. They wanted to disrupt the book launch. Arno doesn't even want to imagine how far they would have gone. The policeman puts a hand on his shoulder. He said he shouldn't worry, thanks to the surveillance camera footage they will find the three of them. Some witnesses who saw the three escape are being questioned at the same time.

In fact, the very next day, the investigators arrest two of the perpetrators: Bernd Larsson and Markus Lenninge. There is no trace of Simon Lummo, who beat one bouncer and injured another with a knife. The arrested men are both from Jyväskylä. The 17-year-old Markus Lenninge testifies that he did not know Simon Lummo. He had followed his friend Markus, who had suggested the "trip" to the public library. There had never been any talk of a violent plan; in that case he would not have joined the other two. Since he himself did not use violence against the bouncers and is a minor, the investigators let him go. Bernd Larsson does not know where Simon Lummo is. After escaping from the building, they parted ways. While searching his apartment and belongings, the officers come across a USB stick with a database of 300 people they created themselves, including photos and personal information. In the process, Lummon divides the people on his USB stick into groups based on ethnicity, religious background and political views. Thus, the investigators find groups called "Jews" or "The Elite."

Li and Mikael comment on the incidents of the previous evening on the same day. The young author praises the audience, because it was only thanks to them that the perpetrators were prevented from entering the hall, thus preventing worse physical violence. Li calls for a just verdict in her statement: "The goal of these people is apparently to make politically motivated violence something normal. For this reason, it is now extremely important that the judiciary stand up for freedom of expression and recognize the political nature of this neo-national socialist attack."

But in January 2014, Simon Lummo is still on the run. The district court arranges for him to be tried in absentia, and the police put a finder's fee on him. Simon Lummo has been considered a fugitive since the attack during the LGBTQ event in July 2012. He has since been identified by the victim and the event organizer as the perpetrator with the pepper spray.

On a cold winter day in November 2014, a man attacks a young mother who is taking her child on an outing to a playground near Helsinki. He knocks her down and steals her purse. Shortly after, police officers arrest Simon Lummo as the perpetrator - a fortunate oversight, because a few weeks later they pick up the mother's real attacker. Simon did not actually attack the woman, but looks very much like the real perpetrator.

The trial of Bernd Larsson and Simon Lummo takes place in January 2015. Lummo is found guilty on all charges, for the pepper spray attack in July 2012 and for the stabbing in the Jyväskylä public library in January 2013. His sentence is 1.5 years' probation. Larsson is sentenced to a fine of 50 daily fines of 300 euros each. In addition, he must pay compensation to all of the 300 people in his personal database, totaling 15,600 USD. For their protection, the police had informed the individuals concerned of their entry in the database, which caused mass panic as no one knew what Larsson intended to do with the information or the individuals themselves.

Lummo's and Larsson's convictions do not constitute a cautionary tale for supporters of the Finnish Resistance Movement. On September 10, 2016, the Nordic Resistance Movement was holding a protest in Helsinki when a young man walked past the group. Jimi Kartonen has nothing but resentment for the radical right-wing ideas and voices his displeasure loudly as he walks by, spitting on the ground in front of the protesters. One of the neo-Nazis then jumps on him and kicks him so hard in the chest that Jimi falls to the ground, hitting his head on the hard concrete of the street. He is observed in the hospital and released after a few days. A week later, he dies as a result of the impact. The attacker is sentenced to 2 years and three months in prison. The whole of Helsinki is in an uproar after this tragic incident and organizes a demonstration against politically motivated violence. 15,000 people take part.

Politicians also react and ban the Finnish Resistance Movement in 2018, as it violates the Finnish Associations Act. According to this, associations may not act against the law and good behavior. The decision is met with criticism, as banning the association interferes with political freedom of expression. Despite protests, the decision to ban the association still stands today.

CHAPTER 14

A strong woman?

(by Heike Schlosser / Keine Gnade – The True Crime Podcast)

Virpi Sanna Sinikka Butt was born in Finland on August 9, 1972. Almost nothing is known about her childhood, but it may not have been as simple and sheltered as one would wish for a child. At the age of 16 she had already given birth for the first time, the boy's father being publicly unknown. Her interests differ from those of girls the same age; Butt's focus is largely on bodybuilding and body worship. In order to achieve her goals, she does not shy away from taking anabolic steroids. But who could have guessed that the athletic young woman would become part of one of the cruelest acts in Finnish criminal history.

The urge to toughen her body beyond natural capabilities quickly becomes an addiction for Virpi Butt. Her consumption of illegal substances increases, and she soon reaches a dose of steroids that exceeds the dosage of an adult man by a factor of ten.

In 1993, her bodybuilding career seemed to have reached its peak. As "Timantti" (English: Diamond), Virpi became part of the TV series "Gladiaattorit", which was also known as "American Gladiator" on international television. In the Finnish version of one of the most successful formats of the 1990s, Butt competes in athletic contests against the show's contestants. She is considered one of the strongest and most powerful gladiators on the series. The 21-year-old is only signed on for the second of three seasons, and so her television career ends after just one year. The once radiant diamond falls prey not only to alcohol, but also to drugs and tranquillisers.

Virpi had her second son in 2000 with the father not being known to the public again. In 2002 she lives with her two sons in a small apartment in Tampere, a large city in the south of Finland. She is well known in the local bars, not only for her excessive drinking, but especially for her fights with other bar patrons. Her violence regularly leads to fights, in which the trained bodybuilder often gets the upper hand against her male opponents. Her brotherly friend Janne Hyvönen is always in on the action. The man, who is three years younger than her spends most of his time with Virpi Butt. Apparently there has never been a sexual relationship between the two, yet Janne plagues herself with jealousy whenever Virpi has a man by her side. This was the case during Virpi's relationship with Kari Pekka Anttonen at the time. The 29-year-old programmer had been friends with Virpi since the 1990s, but the two had lost track of each other. After Anttonen and his girlfriend broke up in 2001, he began drowning his depression, which had intensified as a result, in alcohol. Along the way, the two friends reconnected and not only got to know each other better again, but also fell in love.

On the evening of May 29, 2002, the three friends find themselves in a bar called "Sputnik" after two full nights of heavy drinking. There, too, they are well known, and the alcohol is being consumed in great quantities. Anttonen, who is responsible for paying for the drinks that night, passes out shortly after midnight. The past evenings take their toll. An old bar rule says that if you've already had too much to drink, you'll only bring trouble and no money. So, the trio has to leave the tavern. Butt and Hyvönen carry Anttonen, who keeps slumping, out of the bar. Because of his poor condition, they do not want to go back to his apartment, as they had originally planned. It is located on a hill and is therefore more difficult to reach than Virpi Butt's flat, which is a little further away but easier to reach. Her two children sleep in her apartment, but this is no obstacle for the drunks. In Butt's living room, where her little two-year-old son is sleeping, they continue their lively drinking binge. The 14-year-old boy sleeps in a converted closet in the next room. It is probably around three in the morning when Hyvönen loses control. How exactly the situation escalated is something no one will be able to remember later ... or want to. An argument? A scuffle?

A wrong word? We can only speculate about the motive of the act. The bottom line is that Hyvönen felt provoked. He stabs the unsuspecting Anttonen in the back with a knife. When Anttonen falls forward, Hyvönen sits on his victim and stabs him in the back several times with a second blade. Later he will testify that he felt like a sewing machine when he did this. When Anttonen is miraculously still alive after the excessive attack, Hyvönen slashes his throat with the larger of the two knives and a deep cut. The toddler is in the room the whole time.

Virpi Butt and Janne Hyvönen begin to clean up the bloodstained crime scene. Together they carry Anttonen's body into the bathroom - the task now is to get rid of it as quickly as possible. On the way to the bathroom, they meet Virpi Butt's older son. He remains silent at the sight of the corpse.

In search of a suitable solution for the disposal of the dead body, the murderous friends phone their way through their circle of acquaintances, as neither of them owns a suitable means of transport. No one wants to support them in their operation, because Butt and Hyvönen make no secret of what needs to be transported. However, nobody seems to be taking them seriously because the police don't receive any tips.

They have to find another way out of the situation. Janne Hyvönen goes to his apartment to get some tools. The new plan involves dismembering the body. Back in Virpi Butt's bathroom, the head is now completely severed, the fingertips are cut off, tattoos are removed. At first, the two work with a hunting knife. However, when cutting off the legs at the knees, it proves not to be sharp enough, so a saw is used.

They pack the parts of the body in three garbage bags, which they temporarily store on the balcony of the apartment. Again, Hyvönen tries his luck with a call to his friend. Three garbage bags need to be picked up, he says, and he needs help transporting them. When the friend wants to know what is in the bags, Janne can't help but speak the truth. He had beaten someone to death, he says bluntly on the phone. On that note the desired help wouldn't cooperate and so the sacks remain on the balcony.

After the body parts are not taken from them, the perfidious thoughts of the murderous duo seem to increase immeasurably. Virpi unwraps her dead partner's head again and places it in the kitchen next to the oven to display it like a trophy. Hyvönen, meanwhile, has a very different idea: he takes Anttonen's legs, puts them in the oven "with a little salt and spices," as he later states, and cooks them. He then eats parts of them. His accomplice doesn't join in on the eating. Instead, she calls a friend and asks her to come over. When the friend arrives unsuspectingly, Virpi Butt laughingly presents her with the dead man's head. The friend is horrified and cannot share Butt's humour. This makes Virpi falter as she suddenly realizes the risk of the situation. With some effort, she convinces her friend that it is only the head of a doll, a prop and therefore nothing to worry about. Her friend is reassured, and no report is made to the police.

In the following days, the two show neither sorrow nor doubts for their doing. Driven by pride, they brag about the murder in relevant bars in the city of Tampere. They also make no secret of the fact that the head still adorns Virpi's kitchen. No one believes them. Not even when they show up at a bar with a wet plastic bag, tell the story and claim that the head is inside. Virpi proudly places the sack on a bar stool, swings himself onto the one next to it and puts his feet on the dripping sack. Some visitors decide to leave the bar.

The head has importance to both murderers. While it seems to be the ultimate trophy for Butt, Hyvönen wants to continue to ravage it as if the remains of the dead programmer were his toy. Days later, as he stands in the kitchen once again indulging in alcohol, Hyvönen gets the idea to cook the head. He takes a pan, fills it with water and puts the head in. When the facial features become distorted by the heat and turn into a grinning grimace, Hyvönen laughs. He then removes the head's teeth for no reason, knocking them out, piece by piece. A feeling of complete power flows through Janne Hyvönen. He has murdered, he has dismembered, he has eaten, he is capable of anything.

It almost seems as if Hyvönen and Butt, in their intoxication, have forgotten that the remaining pieces of the corpse are still lying on the balcony of the flat. Inevitably, the bags begin to stink considerably after a while. It is not possible to wait any longer. More calls bring to light an acquaintance who is willing to dispose of the "rubbish". This time the killers do not reveal what the real contents of the bags are. The driver, who will remain anonymous, believes they are hot goods to get rid of, but the smell speaks a different language. Because of the foul stench, the man refuses to drive the bags the planned distance to Nokia, 20 minutes away. Instead, he helps distribute the bags to nearby dumpsters while Virpi and Janne brag about their violent behaviour and laugh at their own numerous jokes. This man, who unintendedly becomes an accomplice, does not go to the police either.

Kari Pekka Anttonen is reported missing. It remains unclear who makes the report to the police, but in the course of the investigation the investigators also knock on the doors of Hyvönen and Butt. As close as the police would be to solving the murder, the interviews do not provide the investigators with any helpful information, there is apparently no reason for an arrest and so both remain at large.

Virpi and Janne's lives return to the usual rut of alcohol and drugs for only a short time. Butt's landlord throws them out of the flat only a short time after the murder. Her alcohol excesses are too extreme, her lifestyle too neglected. Virpi's threats don't help either. She and her children have to move out. The landlord has to have the flat triple-cleaned to put it back into an acceptable condition. The new place is not far from her old home, so Virpi can at least continue to visit her usual bars.

"Midsummer" is traditionally celebrated in Finland in June - a particularly traditional and boisterous festival, with lots of partying and even more drinking. What was originally a pagan celebration in honour of the deity Ukko is now a joyous revelry with good food, bonfires and alcohol.

On 20 June 2003, Janne Hyvönen cares for Virpi Butt's two sons while she goes shopping for alcohol for the upcoming Midsummer. Her path, however, does not lead her to the shopping mall as planned. Instead, she ends up in a bar, as she often does. Here she meets Arto Malinen, a 26-year-old who has lived in Pirkkala near Tampere for three years. The young man has been on a midsummer pub crawl for three days. The two hit it off right away and leave the bar together after closing time at 3:30 am. They take a taxi to Malinen's flat, which they reach shortly after 4:00. Butt pays for the taxi. The two spend a night together, only to start again the next day where they left off: drinking. Together with a friend of Virpi's, who will be called Emma in the following, they visit another bar. The ambience is jolly, there is a lot of laughter and even more drinking. However, after it turns out that Virpi Butt has been banned from the bar because of her past, the group is abruptly forced to leave. On the street they meet a young drug addict, later called Mika, who is looking for a cannabis dealer. They start talking and seem to get on well with each other. The already completely drunk Arto Malinen does not talk back when Butt claims that there is still cannabis in his flat that Mika can buy. The four of them squeeze into a taxi and drive to Malinen's flat in Pirkkala. The taxi ride is not nearly as cheerful as the previous mood would have suggested. Malinen's condition no longer permits any sensible actions. His attempts to kiss Butt are met with violence and disgust on her part. He also falls asleep again and again. Mika is sceptical about Virpi's radical attempts to keep him awake. He finds this extremely violent and strange and obviously feels that it is necessary to calm Virpi Butt down. He offers her diazepam. This is a benzodiazepine that is used for mental agitation such as anxiety disorders or to calm patients before surgery.

When they arrive at Malinen's flat, Emma and Virpi go to the kitchen to have something to eat and more to drink while the two men complete - or try to complete - the drug deal. Malinen, who is drunk beyond belief, hands Mika a packet of matches instead of a box of drugs. That's the last straw for Mika. He feels betrayed and demands 20 USD for a taxi ride back to Tampere. The mood changes abruptly. While Arto Malinen is struggling with a guilty conscience and desperately looking for cannabis to save the situation, Butt finds a knife in the kitchen. She says to Emma, who is about to go to the bathroom, "There'll be another dead body here today." The argument escalates. In desperation, Malinen reaches for Mika's throat, but suddenly falters and cries out: "Damn it, something's stabbed me, damn it, it's burning!" It is in Arto Malinen's back, in up to the handle. The knife Virpi Butt had discovered earlier in the kitchen. With difficulty he pulls it out, staggers and falls forward. The shocked Mika tries to flee, but Virpi holds him back. Under death threats, she forces him to promise that he will not go to the police, then lets the young man go. When Emma comes out of the bathroom, she sees the bleeding Malinen on the floor. He begs for help and an ambulance. Emma also gets scared and wants to leave the flat, but Butt threatens her too. Emma remains at the scene and has to watch as her friend lunges at the victim. She hits the 26-year-old several times and stabs him a total of twelve times. His body is covered in bruises and punctures. Then Virpi Butt drags the man, who had run into her by pure chance less than two days ago, into the bathroom and cuts his throat over the sink.

Just like a year ago, Virpi Butt is now standing in front of the body of a dead man, only this time she is in a different flat. Simply leaving the body there is not an option for her. The dead body must disappear. She calls Janne Hyvönen. He is still in her flat, looking after the children. Emma is now supposed to do the babysitting while Hyvönen helps dispose of the body. Emma sets off for the two children, not without being forcefully informed by Virpi Butt about what will happen to her if she goes to the police first. Hyvönen, on the other hand, sets off for Malinen's flat with knives and a saw in his luggage. "What a midsummer," Hyvönen is still moaning.

Again, the two friends, as if in a frenzy, dismember the corpse. First, they cut off the head, but this time they don't keep it as a trophy. They then remove the fingertips and tattoos. They flush the organs down the toilet. They interrupt the cruel and sweaty procedure again and again. They smoke, drink and recover from the physical exertion. After the body has bled out, they pack it in rubbish bags. They also steal the money and the knife used to murder Malinen from the flat. Then they contact a friend who helps to dispose of the body with a vehicle. Once again, the body parts are distributed among various rubbish bins in the city. For the head, however, they have a special disposal method. They place it in front of the car's tyres so that they can crush it. The attempt fails, however, because the head keeps rolling away.

In the meantime, Emma is very much at peace with the crime, to which she had involuntarily become a witness. Virpi Butt's threat, however, weighs just as heavily on her soul. So instead of calling the police, she calls in a few friends, but they don't believe a word she says.

On the same day, the emergency call centre receives two anonymous calls. The first caller tells of a murder of a man and the dismemberment of the body. The centre thinks this call is a bad joke. After all, it is Midsummer and there is a lot of alcohol being drunk all over the country. Emergency calls are also received in masses, not all of them are to be taken seriously and the emergency call centre is forced to try to distinguish between sincere calls for help and joking reports.

A short time later, another anonymous call comes in. This time it is a female person. She reports having witnessed a murder and that the body has been dismembered. She gives details about the victim and also about the perpetrators.

Although the report is still thought to be a hoax, this time they decide to investigate the tip-off. When the police arrive at Virpi Butt's and Janne Hyvönen's house, it does not take long for the two to make a confession. They willingly lead the investigators to the rubbish bins with the body parts. The duo is arrested on the spot.

In the following interrogations, the two also confess to the murder of Kari Pekka Anttonen. In 2003, countless rubbish bins in the Tampere area are searched in a large-scale search operation. Anttonen's body, however, could not be found and remains are missing to this day.

On 9 September 2003, four people were finally brought to court. Besides Virpi Butt and Janne Hyvönen, Mika and the driver of the car are also accused. The driver for helping to dispose of the body and Mika for not reporting the murder. Emma, on the other hand, is not charged. Her anonymous phone call led to the solving of the case.

The duo is charged with murder and disturbing the peace of the dead; they initially appear indifferent in court. In the further course of the proceedings, they show neither consciousness of guilt nor remorse. Instead, they are conspicuous for their laughter and sarcasm. While Butt wants to blame massive alcohol consumption for the crime, Hyvönen boasts about the feeling of power that the murder of Anttonen, the cannibalism, and dismemberment gave him. It is a great feeling, he says, to simply be above things and capable of anything. The two do not consider the act particularly cruel. They would not have inflicted prolonged suffering on the victims; the killing would have been quick. Even though the assumptions and presumptions are manifold, an assured motive for both acts remains unknown to this day. An expert opinion classifies both delinquents as fully culpable.

On 9 June 2004, the verdict was decided. The driver of the car is sentenced to 3 months in prison, Mika receives a sentence of 30 days in prison. Virpi Butt and Janne Hyvönen receive life sentences.

Virpi Butt, against all recommendations, gets released on 31 December 2018 after 15 years and 5 months in prison. She now lives in Tampere again, under a new name. A short time later, Janne Hyvönen was also released. He, too, is at high risk of re-offending. Nevertheless, both offenders, favoured by good conduct and stable family relationships, are given the chance of reintegration into Finnish society.

Closing words from the author

Dear Reader,

Thank you for holding my book in your hands. This is my sixth book since June 2019, and I invite you to read all the other books in the series as well. Each is a True Crime bestseller.

May I write a few more lines about me?

I write part-time, spending every free minute at my desk, researching, writing, and editing texts. It took me years to find the courage to publish my first book because I got in my own way, as is quite typical. I needed everything to be perfect before I would take the plunge. So many years passed before I finally decided to close the door on perfection and instead told myself, "Only a moving boat can be steered." I wanted to write, publish, and if possible, make a living from it. I acknowledge there may be some flaws in my work. Having a family makes it a more difficult decision, but one well worth it. Maybe one day we'll be able to live off the books entirely. After all, the first book's royalty distribution paid the bill for a family vacation, so that's a good start.

Thank you all for the encouragement that reaches me through your reviews and encourages me to keep writing. To this day, I read, deeply grateful, every single review. If you enjoyed my book, it would delight me to receive a 5-star review from you after finishing it. There's no better way to support me and ensure that many more books in this series are published in the future.

The successful book series
by Adrian Langenscheid

His distinctive style and the success of his books made Adrian Langenscheid one of the most successful true crime authors in Germany. Have you enjoyed this book? If so, feel free to order the other books in the series and encourage other readers to immerse themselves in the world of true crime by writing a review.

Did you like this book? If so, I would love to give you another of my publications as a gift. If interested, please sign up for my "true crime" newsletter. In the future, you will receive spam-free information from me and be able to download the eBook "True Crime Best of Adrian Langenscheid" as a special welcome and thank you.

You can find the newsletter at:
https://www.subscribepage.com/truecrime

or just scan the qr-Code.

Yours sincerely,
Adrian Langenscheid